In **Risky Business,** environmental disasters, our relationship with nature and the Nature archetype are explored from a Jungian perspective through the use of nature myths that illustrate greed and environmental destruction.

Our relationship with nature is considered through a felt-sense of nature's presence, what Jung called the "One World" or *unus mundus.* Using Jung's complex theory and his work on archetypes, the author combines his background working as a scientist for hazardous waste cleanup projects and his training as a Jungian analyst to examine the psychological problem of toxic environmental spills.

Risky Business examines how Jung's theoretical ideas activate the psychology of not only the individual but also the collective when environmental disaster occurs. Specific toxic spill case studies illustrate how the Nature archetype can be expressed within communities that struggle with cleanup; the resolution of conflicts between parties often reveals the presence of what Jung called the Self working at the level of the group.

Finally, the author discusses a love story written by J. R. R. Tolkien, within the framework of an alchemical model, as an allegory for building a resilient and more engaged relationship with nature.

STEPHEN J. FOSTER, Ph.D., M.A., is a graduate of the Inter-regional Society of Jungian Analysts with a private practice in Boulder, Colorado. He holds a Ph.D. in organic chemistry and has an environmental consulting firm where he calculates cleanup levels for hazardous waste sites in the U.S. and around the world.

MARIE-LOUISE VON FRANZ, HONORARY PATRON

Studies in Jungian Psychology
by Jungian Analysts

DARYL SHARP, GENERAL EDITOR

RISKY BUSINESS

A Jungian View of
Environmental Disasters
And the Nature Archetype

STEPHEN J. FOSTER

Library and Archives Canada Cataloguing in Publication

Foster, Stephen J., 1955-
   Risky business : a Jungian view of environmental
   disasters and the nature archetype / Stephen J. Foster

(Studies in Jungian psychology by Jungian analysts ; 130)
Includes bibliographical references and index.
ISBN 978-1-894574-33-4

   1. Environmental psychology. 2. Environmental protection—
Psychological aspects. 3. Jungian psychology. 4. Archetype (Psychology).
I. Title. II. Series: Studies in Jungian psychology by Jungian analysts ; 130

BF353.5.N37F68 2011   155.9'1   C2010-905702-3

INNER CITY BOOKS
Box 1271, Station Q, Toronto, ON M4T 2P4, Canada.
Telephone (416) 927-0355 / Fax (416) 924-1814
Toll-free (Canada and U.S.): Tel. 1-888-927-0355 / Fax 1-888-924-1814
Website: www.innercitybooks.net / E-mail: booksales@innercitybooks.net
Honorary Patron: Marie-Louise von Franz.
Publisher and General Editor: Daryl Sharp.
Senior Editor: Victoria B. Cowan.
Office Manager: Scott Milligan.

INNER CITY BOOKS was founded in 1980 to promote the
understanding and practical application of the work of C. G. Jung.

Cover Image: "Greeting the Day," photo of Harrington Pond by Irene
Miller, Stratford, Ontario, Canada (website: www.imillerphoto.com).

Printed and bound in Canada by Thistle Printing Limited

CONTENTS

See final pages for other Inner City titles

List of Figures

Acknowledgments

While it often seems a cliché to acknowledge so many people, it is my lived experience that these types of projects do not happen without support and without outside influence and encouragement.

I want to thank my parents, who are no longer on this earth, because they lived a life that depended upon the seasons of nature. I am grateful to my four sisters who never let me forget the feminine that surrounds us.

Throughout this work, and through most of my life, my partner, Nora Swan-Foster, has been a constant companion and support to me. I would like to acknowledge and thank her for her presence in my life, her help with this book, and so much more.

Charles Rees, CBE, my organic chemistry professor, was a dynamic force in my early professional life, and opened my mind to ways of exploring the alchemical mystery of the invisible world.

I want also to acknowledge and thank my friend and colleague Jeffrey Kiehl for our ongoing discussions and collaboration on nature and the environment, and that journey to Orodruin.

Jennifer Phelps offered her editorial assistance and enthusiastic support for this manuscript that otherwise have remained a thesis collecting dust. And certainly this book could not have come about without the many Jungian analysts who have guided me on this journey, including my publisher, Daryl Sharp. Thank you.

Lastly, this book is dedicated to my adult children, Fiona and Hamilton, and to the children of the future who will no doubt be forced to take up this challenge of finding a "right relationship" with nature.

On the whole, it is my hope that this book will do its part in raising our consciousness about the role nature plays in our lives and how fragile we humans are in her presence.

Preface

We need more psychology. We need more understanding of human nature, because the only real danger that exists is man himself. He is the great danger, and we are pitifully unaware of it. We know nothing of man, far too little. His psyche should be studied, because we are the origin of all coming evil.[1]

This book explores the Nature archetype and humankind's relationship to it over time. It is a timely piece of work because the externalization (dumping) of pollution onto nature is causing significant and possibly irreversible environmental damage. I am writing as oil from the Transocean Ltd. oilrig, rented by BP, washes onto the shores of Mississippi, Alabama and Louisiana. Scenes of this disaster on television evoke memories of the Exxon Valdiz and the Torrey Canyon, which are rapidly becoming our modern-day myths.

Just as many creation myths document the advent of humanity's self-awareness or consciousness, other myths document how humanity has exploited nature for its resources since the beginning of time, participating in various forms of environmental destruction.

In modern times, the Act of Enclosure in England moved rural populations from the countryside to the cities, thus separating an agrarian society from nature. The Industrial Revolution started the modern era of pollution and environmental damage. I shall relate three case studies of environmental damage to modern expressions of the Nature archetype. These cases reflect the wider threat to the earth's ecosystems: global climate change. They also illustrate the impact of modern industrial society and environmental damage, as well as individual acts of imagination, creativity and courage in the process of cleanup. These are expressions of what C. G. Jung called the Self. In Jungian terminology, this book ex-

---

[1] C. G. Jung, "The Face to Face Interview with John Freeman," BBC television, October 1959, in *C.G. Jung Speaking,* p. 436.

plores the shadow aspects of humanity's relationship with nature and explores possible reasons for our lack of response on local, national and global levels.

The Nature archetype is bipolar, being expressed through its instinctual pole in the body through sexual, aggressive and protective behaviors and biological processes, and through its spiritual pole in a deeply felt connection to nature. The alchemists called this felt-sense of nature *unus mundus*, or One World. Their theory of our connection to nature is explored through analogy with J. R. R. Tolkien's story, "The Lay of Leithian," from *The Silmarillion*.

Introduction

Children brought up in the country, as Jung was, do start with a certain advantage over city children, in that they have every opportunity from an early age to face up to life as it is, to its dark side as well as its light.[2]

I see the Nature archetype as ancient, vast and pervasive. Every other archetype in the human psyche comes out of it or is connected to it, including the Great Mother or feminine archetypes, and the Great Father or masculine archetypes. I believe it is a universal life force that has both physical form (earth, seas, mountains, etc.) and psychological power (it activates both instinctual and spiritual drives). The focus of this book is on the small fraction of the archetype that relates to the externalization (that is, dumping) of industrial and anthropogenic wastes onto the environment.

In this book, I refer to the physical form of the Nature archetype as "nature." Within the idea of these physical forms, words such as *environment, ecosystem, country* and *earth* all conjure different images, and for the purpose of this book "nature" represents the varied physical forms of the Nature archetype. It includes those parts of the world where human settlements have not invaded natural ecosystems, or where sufficient area (land or water) exists to be self-sustaining. It is diverse and free from significant human impact, so it could also be called wilderness or pristine land. I also use nature to represent the place where we might connect to the Nature archetype in a personal way, a locale where we personally have a connection to the land, sea or woods and feel a sense of tranquility and wholeness. It is where we connect to the sense of the place itself, or in Latin the *genius loci.*

Nature is also found in parks, greenways or open spaces, harbors or ponds that co-exist in an urban area. These areas support a wide range of species, most of which are acclimatized to the presence of people. Al-

---

2 Barbara Hannah, *Jung: His Life and Work, a Biographical Memoir,* pp. 25f.

10

though open space is valuable to a city, it is usually too small to avoid human impact, so it cannot support the diverse ecological populations consistent with pre-industrial times. Nevertheless, for individuals who grow up close to this type of environment, it may provide a sense of the physical aspect of the Nature archetype, that is, a connection to nature that has meaning.

Nature is also a term used to represent the earth's projected or personified feminine soul-like form, or *anima mundi*. Humanity is part of this natural world and the Nature archetype is expressed, in part, through humanity. The *genius loci*, sense of a place, is both unique to a specific location and common to all places in its meaning and connection, through felt experience of a greater universe. The alchemists referred to this experience as *unus mundus*, One World.

Our deep and meaningful connection to nature often has what Jung called a numinosity; that is, it is filled with a supernatural or spiritual presence. Jung also believed that numinous experiences indicate the presence of the Self, and are often called a religious experience. Therefore, the Nature archetype is a mode of expression of the Self, or the energy that flows through the Self into human consciousness. I use a capital letter in "Nature archetype" because of this connection to the Self.

Humanity became self-aware while in the presence of nature, so human consciousness has always been influenced by the presence of the Nature archetype. As a species we are often myopic, believing that the earth is here for our use alone. The reverse may be true. We may be experiencing a Copernican moment in humanity's ecological and species development, that is, a discovery that we are here to serve the earth and not the other way around. We rarely consider the world from the perspective of the archetype. According to Jung's archetypal theory, archetypes have instinctual and spiritual poles that are deeply embedded in the personal and collective psyche. Science attempts to study nature. The spiritual pole of the Nature archetype is a mystery, and the archetype may have a *telos*, or direction, of which we remain unaware. Yet, from time to time, the psyche may catch a glimpse of the spiritual dimension of the psyche through nature. From the perspective of the Nature archetype, humanity may be like the dinosaur—expendable—another step in an evolutionary or divine strategy (or both). And nature's response is a call to consciousness for mankind.

The particular interest of this book is the aspect of the Nature archetype that relates to humanity's overuse of nature's resources and the dumping of anthropogenic wastes back into nature. If earth were considered a single organism, the changes effected by wastes in nature might be considered a feedback mechanism. These effects may also be considered an expression of the Nature archetype attempting to bring about a shift in human consciousness.

At the beginning of civilization, it was common to damage the environment through dumping and overuse. Today, in many ways we are still unconscious of the degree to which we dump waste into nature, or we are aware of it but have agreed to accept it as the price of modern life, without regard to nature. Is this part of our genetic makeup? When we were living in what Lucien Lévy-Bruhl called *participation mystique,* "a state of identity in mutual unconsciousness" with our environment,[3] it was a natural/normal part of our hunter/gatherer societies to use, dump and move on. Our consciousness was not as developed and daily life was simpler. Now, in this modern era, we do not physically move to find new food sources or to avoid our wastes, but it is still in our human psyche to think that nature can handle our wastes and excesses.

Neuroscience has shown that the human brain has parts that deal with lower order emotional and physiological activities, and beneath the high functioning brain lays a remnant of our ancestral brain. Psychology has demonstrated the presence of both higher order defenses, such as intellectualization, rationalization, dissociation and displacement, and more primitive defenses of denial, distortion and splitting. These personal defense mechanisms appear to be working on a collective level to prevent a clear recognition of environmental problems and remedial action. As a result of our behaviors, we are now faced with serious conflicts between our continued drive for "advancement" and our earth's need to survive.

A short section of this book provides a summary of how the non-Jungian world is working on the psychology of environmental problems.

---

[3] See "Mind and Earth," *Civilization in Transition,* CW 10, par. 69. (CW refers throughout to C. G. Jung, *The Collected Works)*

Consistent with cognitive psychology and other psychologies that exclude the collective unconscious, the focus is on the present moment and typically limited to our own personal denial system. When we think of global climate change, or staunching BP's gusher in the gulf, we are overwhelmed, suffer impotent rage or deny the problem. We seem particularly good at ignoring deep-seated intuitive feelings, and even more concerning is that we ignore or reject convincing scientific evidence. In this book, I summarize the work of ego psychologists who have pondered this question and the associated psychological defense mechanisms, such as denial, intellectualization, etc. However, from a Jungian perspective, we are being charged to undertake a significant amount of shadow work, that is, the work of bringing to consciousness unpleasant, repressed or unwanted psychological material concerning the continued destruction of nature and the environment. Environmental shadow work, becoming conscious of our current impacts on nature, should be both individual and collective.

In addition, I suggest that, as a result of our own personal psychological defensive reactions and unconscious response to traumatic events, we are preconditioned to activate an archetypal defense mechanism that has been identified in early childhood trauma, as described in the work of Donald Kalsched.4 His model provides a useful paradigm for understanding the barriers that create a reluctance to deal with this deep-seated issue.

Is nature rising up and talking back to us, forcing us at this point in time to work against our human propensity in order to be in relationship *with* nature? It is as if we were oscillating between our old habit of polluting and a new consciousness of the need to clean up the environment and steward nature. Both aspects seem to be works *contra naturam,* against human nature.

History and mythology show us that we have gone through cycles of use and abuse of nature before. However, because of industrialization on a global scale, we cannot continue this uncontrolled behavior. Now we are discovering that nature is responding to our large-scale environ-

---

4 See, for instance, The Inner World of Trauma: Archetypal Defenses of the Personal Spirit, also Thomas Singer and Samuel Kimbles, The Cultural Complex, p. 18.

mental pollution through climate change. When we are open to it, we see that these changes have impacted our daily lives. For example, in Colorado, where I live, the summers are hotter, the pine beetles are moving through the pine woods unchecked due to warmer winters, and the snows are less predictable and often of lower volume. Unfortunately, most people do not recognize any change, and what one is unaware of one cannot change.

We should be concerned about such issues because subtle changes in seasonality upset the delicate balance and interconnectedness of nature. Changes in ice flow pattern mean polar bears cannot reach feeding grounds in the spring, leading to starvation of their young, and subsequent species loss. The vectors carrying disease, such as mosquitoes carrying malaria that can now reach the cities that were previously out of reach and the shift in cycles is contributing to the sixth extinction, a period of species loss unseen since the fifth extinction occurred sixty-five million years ago.[5]

We cannot know the ultimate goal of the Nature archetype. As with all archetypes, we can only see how it is expressed in the world by us, or how it expresses itself through us. And it is unclear how pollution, on a scale the earth has never seen before, fits within the purpose and scope of the Nature archetype.

In the time since Enclosure and the Industrial Revolution, humanity has changed its relationship with the earth forever. We cannot go back to pre-industrial conditions, except perhaps through catastrophe. The extraction of natural resources and the externalization (dumping) of the wastes and byproducts from human industrial development into the environment have always been an integral part of industry. Only recently, in developed countries, has dumping been partly legislated against to prevent the indiscriminate dumping of waste chemicals into the environment. On a collective level, the problem of the externalization by dumping seems insurmountable. However, it has been my experience that changes in an individual's awareness of nature can, in fact, bring about changes in both personal and collective consciousness. As Jung repeatedly suggests, a new personal consciousness infects and transforms col-

---

[5] See Richard Leaky and Roger Lewin, *The Sixth Extinction.*

lective consciousness, so I believe that ultimately, an individual's relationship with nature may transform the collective.

Dumping waste into our Commons, that is, into our seas, rivers, lakes and air, continues relatively unabated in the United States. Recently, these practices have been outsourced to less regulated countries. Uncontrolled disposal is almost completely accepted as standard practice in the developing world. Why does humanity accept this? As individuals we know better, so why does the collective allow it: probably because it is archetypal. If this is true, dumping would play a role in the Nature archetype, but what role? If there is an underlying direction or purpose to a Nature archetype, where is it going and what is the *telos* of it for our time? Is its purpose as simple as evoking human relationship on a collective level, an Eros factor? These are difficult questions, akin to asking the goals and purpose of God, and impossible to answer. My response to these questions is mere speculation because an archetype can only be observed in reflection, or through experience. Consistent with archetypal theory, however, I believe there is archetypal bipolarity, with the potential positive purpose of raising consciousness, although it may be a race for consciousness before environmental damage is too grave.

We cannot observe the Nature archetype directly. We observe archetypes through images, symbols and the effects they exert on us. What are we observing about this particular archetype at the present time? If it is acting through us and upon our environment to make something conscious, what does it want or need to express so urgently? These difficult questions will be explored throughout this book.

Similar to the initial aspects of personal analysis, recognition of collective shadow behaviors is key to the initial phases of dealing with environmental damage. We must recognize how emissions impact our global air and water quality, or how ocean dumping affects not only those adjacent to the seas, but anyone who eats fish. In human relationships, when we recognize the contrasexual "other" within, it allows for a deeper relationship with others. This is also an important first step in developing a relationship with the earth as (m)other. Nature is often equated with "Mother Earth" because (like a mother) the earth provides food, a home and resources, as well as receiving human wastes for millennia. I discuss this analogy because it represents a predominant personification in the human psyche. As a good mother, nature was able to tolerate and metabolize these wastes for the most part. But we are now able to produce wastes more rapidly than nature can process them. As a result, nature's balance has been thrown off and many species are declining at an alarming rate.

On a conscious level, we may be unaware of species loss, and not care particularly much about what is happening many miles from home, but somewhere, on an unconscious level, we feel the loss and we are diminished. We possess a particular knowing that future generations will not experience the power and majesty of the polar bear on the ice, or the tiger in the jungle, or the whale in the ocean. As Jung notes, "Nature is not matter only, she is also spirit."[6] He has implied that a loss of connection to nature causes a loss of vitality and a loss of soul.[7]

In addition, due to overpopulation and the needs that come with an increase in the number of people on the earth, we might consider mankind a weed in nature's garden that is choking out all other species. Overpopulation is indeed one of *the* root causes of our environmental problems, and the religious attitude of "go forth and multiply," which is present in some form in most religions, is impacting the earth in a significant way. Over the past century the sheer number of people on the earth has passed beyond the sustaining capacity of our planet. We must develop a collective consciousness that reduces and maintains the number of people on the earth at a sustainable level. In this case, sustainable means the number of people that can be fed, clothed and transported, and whose wastes the earth can process, with less than one year's solar energy. Fueled by the archetypal (biological) need to have sufficient numbers of people to survive as a species, we now reproduce without much regard for the consequences on nature. Although this issue has a significant effect on nature, population is not discussed at length in this book. Meanwhile, nature herself may be acting in this regard through floods, earthquakes, firestorms, hurricanes, etc.

It remains to be seen if we can respond to our current environmental

---

6 See "Paracelsus as a Spiritual Phenomenon," *Alchemical Studies,* CW 13, par. 229.

7 C. G. Jung Letters, vol. 2, p. 626.

situation and transcend the psychological barriers of the shadow (unconscious dumping) and power (unbridled greed) complexes. These attitudes have dominated recent history, but if worked through, humanity may become aware of the Nature archetype and thereby attain a deeper level of environmental consciousness and a new relationship with nature.

Nature has been a continuous place of solace and renewal for me throughout my life. Chapter One is a description of this relationship and how nature supports me in my individuation journey. In Chapter Two, I provide a framework and background to Jung's structure of the psyche, including complexes, archetypes and the Self. The Nature archetype, like all archetypes, is bipolar; one side drives the expression of instinct (a will to survive) and the other is a spiritual drive for creative expression. Many of our current problems with the externalization of waste could be viewed as a lack of consciousness of these poles. Jung's theory also includes the Self, an image of wholeness within the psyche of each of us, and yet connected to all. Through a felt-sense of what the alchemists call *unus mundus*, or One World, I believe we experience an aspect of the Self that flows through the collective unconscious and connects us with each other and the Nature archetype.

Also in Chapter Two, I explore Jung's theory of complexes and the concept of shadow, on a personal and collective level. In particular, I see humanity's collective propensity to dump hazardous wastes into the environment as a shadow problem. There are many psychological parallels between processing pollution and revealing shadow issues in Jungian analysis. However, I am less interested in uncovering the personal shadow in this book. Instead I focus on how waste, as the collective shadow, is externalized onto the earth, thus making it a worldwide problem. I suggest that there may be archetypal defenses in place that are barriers to change. Jungian psychology, particularly the analysis of myth and stories, provides tools for us to examine shadow issues related to the domination of nature and the externalization of waste.

In Chapter Three, I explore selected early Greek and nature myths that bring our behaviors to consciousness. Humanity's awareness of itself is expressed in creation mythology. Due to the large number of nature myths, I have narrowed my perspective in an attempt to identify a particular thread of the Nature archetype. Creation mythology describes the emergence of human consciousness out of a fused state with nature. When examining creation myths, I view them from the current, somewhat patriarchal position that nature has been assigned feminine attributes because of her container-like qualities and because of her bounty that sustains humanity. This is simply a viewpoint for this book supported by Jung, Neumann and others. However, nature can also be seen as having masculine attributes, because in reality nature has both masculine and feminine aspects, and is gender equal. I also look at myths that illustrate humanity's historical attitude of dominance over and destruction of nature: the myth of Gilgamesh and the myth of Erysichthon. Both of these myths warn us against an attitude of destructive arrogance. Pentheus, in the Dionysian myth, also illustrates a certain attitude toward nature that is still present today.

In Chapter Four, I explore the impact of specific modern historical events, such as Enclosure and the Industrial Revolution. As cultivation produced an excess of food, it allowed for the development of culture, the written word, science and eventually industrialization. This has fueled increased human reproduction, exploration, overuse of the earth's resources, and mass uncontrolled dumping of by-products.

Exploration of our current experience of the Nature archetype is reinforced in Chapter Five through three current case studies of environmental pollution. I discuss how they have impacted nature and the individual's response to the Nature archetype through the process of cleaning up these waste sites. Science in the twenty-first century shows that humanity is degrading nature. Through films such as *An Inconvenient Truth* and *The 11th Hour*, *Gasland*, etc., we directly see the changes and destruction we have wrought; so why are we not outraged and motivated to change the way we live now and in the future in order to reduce the impact on our environment? And what might it take to bring about a change in consciousness?

I suggest that specific psychological defense mechanisms may be operating to prevent collective societal change. Jung's psychology can be used to reframe the problem and conceptualize images of renewal. At the core of Jung's work is the idea that symbols can unite the conscious and the unconscious, and expand the ego, allowing the incorporation of concepts that we may have defended against. He also suggested the use of human imagination as a means to connect to the Self and bring about change. In a small way, these case studies show how an individual who has imagination and is connected to the Self can make a difference both locally and collectively. These case studies also show the infectious power of the group process that enhances dialogue and relationship, which is needed to overcome feelings of isolation, futility and despair. Eros, or feeling relationship, supports the needed transformation.

Science is predicting a range of scenarios for the earth that are catastrophic for humanity. Nevertheless, we must develop a new consciousness of our interactions with and impact on nature. I refer to this as a "Nature-consciousness." A key part of this Nature-consciousness is that it represents a serious "I-Nature" relationship. When Martin Buber talked of an "I-Thou" relationship, he was describing that of the individual with an "Other," and because of his personal belief system he ultimately saw the Other as God.[8] In an I-Nature relationship we would treat nature as an earthly representation of the Other, deserving respect in our everyday world, and we would relate to it seriously because of its I-Thou interaction. This requires dialogs with nature and with others about nature. With dialog we would become conscious of nature and our direct and indirect effects on her. The dialog would also bring the archetype closer to consciousness.

The advent of the atomic age has profoundly affected the human psyche. It is perhaps only a matter of time before the loss of species, loss of coastal cities and impacts on food sources will, like the atomic bomb, also affect human consciousness. However, environmental disasters stimulate denial, fear and anxiety. With the right leadership, and an emphasis on prioritizing pollution reduction, clean water, soil and air, and reversing climate change, there is potential for transformation. This will involve using creativity and imagination if the changes are to be timely and far reaching.

The spiritual alchemist Gerhard Dorn developed a process that may be used as a model. He suggests that entering into a relationship with nature

---

8 See Ronald Gregor Smith, trans., *Martin Buber: I and Thou.*

could lead to a more positive outcome for humanity than science is currently predicting. In Chapter Six, I explore Dorn's model. Further, and much like alchemy, fiction (particularly science fiction/fantasy) is a means through which unconscious material illustrating potential alternative worlds are projected into society. Science fiction can portray situations that attempt to come to grips with our relationship with nature through imaginative scenarios and futuristic worlds.

This is a broad topic, so in Chapter Six I also discuss futuristic stories that illustrate humanity's potential relationship with nature through the world of mythopoetic-fiction. I discuss a story of love and relationship in the writings of J. R. R. Tolkien, to illustrate alternative approaches to our relationship with nature. The "Lay of Leithian," from his book *The Silmarillion,* is used as an example for discussion and interpretation of Dorn's alchemical model. I see the beautiful "Lay of Leithian" as a simple amplification of the alchemical process and a personified story of how we might connect to a greater universe or *unus mundus*. This connection offers humanity a pathway into relationship with the Nature archetype and the possibility for transformation of consciousness. The story also suggests that some specific tools such as discernment, imagination and creativity are needed to liberate our collective selves from the current oppression of unsustainable and even destructive technologies. The story intimates that the Self must be involved in the outcome.

Modern industrialized society is beginning to recognize environmental problems. On a collective level, there are many ideas for change. However, these ideas often become polarized into opposites. On one side, there are those who suggest that a mythic view of the world be adopted and mankind return to a pre-industrial attitude (abandoning "progress" and modern technologies). On the other side, there are those who argue that whatever problems we may have can be resolved with scientific advances. C. G. Jung's ideas suggest that the tension of the opposites, if held long enough, will result in the intervention of the Self through the transcendent function, producing a transcendent symbol and leading to an expanded consciousness.

Over the past twenty-five years I have engaged in environmental work, evaluating hazardous waste sites in the United States and elsewhere. Through this work I have seen what I believe are manifestations of the Self, appearing especially in the form of imagination, to create transcendent symbols. Where contamination requires cleanup, an individual or group may have an idea of what they believe best works for their local environment. Typically this solution is in the service of nature.

There are many possible outcomes to our current environmental problems. The earth may survive, but will humanity adapt and allow the Nature archetype to change our consciousness without radically affecting the physical aspects of nature?

It is clear to me that society will not look the same in a few years from now. I believe that Jung's analytical psychology can provide a psychological framework for the changes and adjustments that are needed. The key, however, is consciousness of our own psychology, understanding of our own and collective shadow, and a willingness to be open to the energy felt as *unus mundus*.

1
Personal Background

And we go out as the fish go out, leaving the taste
Of the rivers we know, joining the dark invisible weight
Of what we would become, the calm sense of movement
Seeing the others forming our shoals, and the scales
On our sides filling the depth with trembling stars.[9]

Nature is and has always been an important presence in my life. Born and raised in rural Sussex, in what is known as one of the Home Counties of England, I realize how nature influenced my life from the very beginning. These Counties near London provided the food for the city when horse and cart were the only means of transportation. The Counties near London were the gardens that provided fresh food for the city.

The county of Sussex is made up of rolling green hills of oak and chestnut trees. It is protected, much like selected towns in the U.S., by a green space law that prevents building on any land that has not previously contained a structure. My village, Bodiam,[10] is a rural hamlet in the ancient Weald (from an Indo-European root meaning "forest" or "wild")[11] with the River Rother running through it. My surname, Foster, is derived from "forester," someone who works with trees. Trees and rivers have always been important symbols for me.

In Roman times, Bodiam was a wharf town with a villa and Roman garrison because the river was connected to the sea. Following the Norman invasion of Saxon England, in 1066, Bodiam became a Castle Village with a fortified house on the edge of Romney Marsh. In 1291, St. Giles church was built on the top of the hill so that it could be seen by the church on the hill of the next village, and so on. As a child I played in

---

[9] David Whyte, *River Flow.*

[10] See wikipedia.org/wiki/Bodiam.

[11] See *Oxford English Dictionary,* compact edition, p. 3718..

the castle and prayed in the church. These buildings and this history provided a common experience to all who lived there. More importantly, to me the countryside became a place of refuge from the chaos of my family and the rural poverty in which we lived.

When possible, I spent my life outside in nature. As an infant my mother would wheel me in a "pram" into the hop fields (the major employer in the village being the Guinness Brewery that farmed hops for their beer) and leave me in nature, or in the arms of Mother Nature, while she worked the hop fields through the spring, summer and into the great autumn harvest. The Great Mother was always present when my personal mother was not, and it was the presence of nature that supported me when I needed to escape. It provided both a physical and psychological refuge for me. I would leave the turmoil of my home to play in and around the oak trees where a stream of water left the castle moat, or I would fish in the river with the kingfishers as the sun came up during the long summer days. At that time in the morning, the mist over the river felt timeless and sparked rich imaginings and fantasies that have stayed with me all of my life.

I would lose myself for hours in this environment, feeling the silky water on my skin when I swam in the river or the soft grass under foot on the field near where the sheep grazed. Nature was always present when I began hating the restrictions of my village and tried to leave as an adolescent. My personal experience of nature came through a felt sense. As I describe later, Jung talks of this felt-sense phenomenon using the term *unus mundus*, the alchemical concept of One World, where one feels a profound and spiritual connection to the world throughout the body. This was *my* foundational experience of nature. Psychologically, we might say that I became merged with nature. It is one of the most important ways by which humans connect to nature. A felt-sense connection to nature forms the basis for many shamanic practices, and I will briefly discuss this type of connection later.

I believe we have all had these kinds of experiences, even if we grew up in a town or city. Because of my personal experience of nature, I am interested in how we as a species have moved from the psychological condition in which we lived as children, a state of being one with nature, unconsciously fused, in *participation mystique*,[12] to a state where we use and abuse nature without apparent regard for the outcome. We seem to have developed an attitude of superiority over or a need to control nature. How does this shift occur, and how did we, do we, go from a state of fusion to one of relative disregard?

Eventually, I crossed the bridge over the river from my village to the world outside. At eighteen, I left home and found a job. I worked for a couple of years before realizing I could go to college. In the towns and cities where I received my education, I found society to be very stimulating. Unconsciously, I sought a profession that would allow me to understand how nature worked, and eventually would use this education to work with nature and the savages of industrial man. Initially, I learned organic chemistry because it is one of the fundamental sciences that shows how the underlying processes of life work. With the encouragement and support of my wife, and the needs of my anima, I have been actively working on environmental issues since 1981. For the past thirty years, I have been a part of the small group of scientists who conduct human and environmental risk assessments at hazardous waste sites.

Specifically, I calculate the risks to human and ecological life from the hazardous chemicals dumped, illegally or with the permission of society, into the environment. This work is about searching for the "wounds" to the earth, assessing their severity and establishing a plan for treatment and healing. It is shadow work. The profession can be compared to an environmental emergency response physician in terms of the urgency of deadlines, the structure of regulations, and the need to evaluate the health of various ecosystems to see if they can be cleaned up and so kept alive.

In this work, I often lead multi-leveled negotiation processes that involve dialog among the public and the polluter, explain data and communicate risk at town meetings. I have witnessed first-hand environmental devastation in Europe, Africa and the Americas, giving me access to different cultures, various levels of environmental consciousness and a range of personal reactions. Many of the stories of devastation are emotionally and intellectually overwhelming, and consume years of continuous teamwork. They are essentially all complex shadow stories or ac-

---

[12] "The Transformation of Libido," *Symbols of Transformation,* CW 5, par. 204.

counts of materials dumped unconsciously, sometimes over many years, without thought or regard for the future impact on others.

I am writing this as oil flows unabated into the Gulf of Mexico from the ruptured well drilled by the BP-Trans-Oceanic oilrig that exploded in May 2010. I believe the damage from this spill will be seen as one of the greatest American environmental catastrophes ever, and I hope it will become a catalyst for environmental change in Nature-consciousness in the U.S. and elsewhere.

I feel a common bond between my own connection to nature and Jung's relationship with nature, including his personal love of the outdoors, of camping and hiking in the mountains, and his fascination with natural life. I also find myself committed, as he was, to understanding the collective relationship between nature and the psyche, and how the Nature archetype expresses itself through the psyche. Nature is the physical world, and yet, the Nature archetype runs through the psyche. It exerts pressure on the psyche, which in turn responds symbolically and metaphorically. And I am interested in how nature psychology works on a collective level, and why it appears different from our personal relationship with nature. In personal psychology, almost every dream has a setting or environment that relates to nature. However, I believe one can occasionally see an archetype more clearly when looking at collective material rather than personal material.

I believe we all respond to the Nature archetype on some level. Some are more responsive to shifts in nature than others. I also believe, like Jung, that shifts in the personal psyche affect the collective, and by improving our personal relationship with nature we can change our collective consciousness about nature. However, what we don't know about we cannot care about. By being open to the needs of nature, and to the Nature archetype, we may become more responsive to it.

3
Archetypes, Complexes and Nature

Archetypes are systems of readiness for action, and at the same time images and emotions. They are inherited with the brain structure—indeed they are its psychic aspect. They represent, on the one hand, a very strong instinctive conservatism, while on the other hand they are the most effective means conceivable of instinctive adaptation. They are thus, essentially, the chthonic portion of the psyche. . . .that portion through which the psyche is attached to nature.[13]

How are we connected to nature? What is the Nature archetype? Why do certain images, particularly those of nature, hold so much energy for us? And how does our feeling response to nature seem to flow into us in some way? The following comments by Jung summarize his position.

As far as we can see, the collective unconscious is identical with Nature to the extent that Nature herself, including matter, is unknown to us. I have nothing against the assumption that the psyche is a quality of matter or matter the concrete aspect of the psyche, provided that "psyche" is defined as the collective unconscious. In my opinion the collective unconscious is the preconscious aspect of things on the "animal' or instinctive level of the psyche. Everything that is stated or manifested by the psyche is an expression of the nature of things, whereof man is a part.[14]

Jung talked of archetypes as an inherited mode of psychic functioning, corresponding to a priori, innate patterns of animal behavior.[15] A number of post-Jungians have reviewed Jung's ideas. Jung's hypothesis of archetypes states they have two poles: an instinctual pole and a spiritual pole. Genetic research has demonstrated that there is an inherited basis for some psychological disorders.[16] Further, this paper shows that inherited psychological disorders are also influenced by environmental factors.

---

[13] "Mind and Earth," *Civilization in Transition,* CW 10, par. 53.

[14] *C. G. Jung Letters,* vol. 2, p. 540.

[15] "Medicine and Psychotherapy," *The Practice of Psychotherapy,* CW 16, par. 206.

[16] R. Plomin, M. J. Owen and McGuffin, "The Genetic Basis of Complex Human Behaviors. In *Science,* vol. 264, pp. 733ff., 1994.

Current genetic and psychological research is oriented towards abnormal behavior and psychopathology, or the instinctual pole of the archetype, rather than the spiritual pole. Although genetic and psychological research does not categorically prove Jung's theory of archetypes at this point, we should stay open to the possibility that current and future research will confirm that symbolic information is carried in the genetic code. In 2002, Anthony Stevens, evolutionary psychiatrist and Jungian analyst, reiterated his support for the idea that the genetic code can carry both symbolic information and the potential for symbolic experience.[17]

Jung's Structure of the Psyche

A schematic illustration of Jung's concept of the human psyche is shown in Figure 1 (modeled on the images and information presented by his colleague Jolande Jacobi).[18] Jung sees the psyche as a partially open sys-

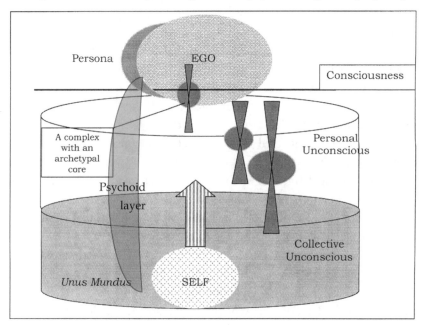

Figure 1. Schematic representation of Jung's concept of the psyche.

17 Stevens, Archetype Revisited, p. 53.
18Jolande Jacobi, *The Psychology of C.G. Jung,* pp. 6, 34, 37, 41, 130.

tem consisting of the sum of the personal and collective unconscious. He describes the ego as the seat of consciousness interacting with the world through personas or masks that show the world who we would like them to see. The ego retains memory and our sense of history of ourselves, and yet is also able to separate out our more negative experiences or images of who we do not want to be and repress them by placing them into the unconscious, relegated to what Jung referred to as the shadow. Further, Jung notes that the ego both directs conscious actions and expresses the goals and directions of the Self, archetype of wholeness in the psyche.[19]

Jung's early experiments with the word association experiment showed that the personal unconscious contains "complexes"—affect-laden psychological factors linked to or containing images that when activated or "constellated" can influence or take over the ego. Jung theorized that complexes have an archetypal core; that is, the ego is linked not just to the personal unconscious, but also to the collective unconscious, where we are linked both to each other and to the collective history of humankind. Jung also theorized that the ego itself is a complex whose archetypal core is the Self. In the psyche, the Self is a paradox, being both the circumference and the regulating center of the psyche.[20] The Self is an *Imago Dei*, or an image of God, the Divine in the human psyche. However, the Self is not God, it is a mystery. The Self is a psychological factor connected to the collective unconscious. The Self can also be seen as connected to a life force that flows from deep in the universe of space and time, through the solar system into our world. As a psychological factor it also connects us to all life.

The Nature archetype has a psychological component that is also connected to the Self, the core of which is connected to a universal force both within and beyond the earth that transcends our comprehension. Nature is made up of our richly diverse environments and we are connected to all aspects of it, visible and invisible. In the psyche, the core of this affect is the Nature archetype, with an instinctual pole and a spiritual pole. To be clear, the Nature archetype is not the Self, but simply an as-

---

19 "The Self," *Aion,*CW 9ii, pars. 43ff.
20 "Individual Dream Symbolism in Relation to Alchemy," *Psychology and Alchemy,* CW 12, par. 44.

pect of the Self, expressed in our psychological environments, and connected, through feeling, to our physical environment.

Complexes

It is important to understand Jung's complex theory relative to the Nature archetype because complexes motivate how we unconsciously act and react to the world, in this case the natural world. Our autonomous complexes, when constellated, act outside of the conscious control of the ego. We all have complexes related to nature, to the environment, to the hazardous chemicals we release into it, and to the effects these chemicals have on the living planet.

Jung developed his complex theory early in his career while working at the Burgholzli mental hospital in Zurich. His then director, Eugene Bleuler, asked him to undertake the word association experiment with normal subjects and schizophrenic patients. These experiments measured response times after asking for an association to a list of words. He found that individuals had longer response times to some words, or the word stimulated bodily reactions.

Jung defined a complex as an autonomous collection of feeling-toned images. Jacobi explicates:

> Jung defines complexes as "psychic entities that have escaped from the control of consciousness, and split off from it to lead a separate existence, in the dark sphere of the psyche from whence they may at any time hinder or help the conscious performance." [21]

Jung theorized that the subjects' reactions were "complex" indicators, meaning that the word has an association to an image in the unconscious, which holds psychic energy, and so indicates where there is loaded affect held in the unconscious. Complexes also show potential conflicts between conscious and unconscious attitudes. Jungian analyst Hans Dieckmann proposes that these "psychic entities" stem from two original ones: "In my judgment all the other complexes can be derived from these two great fundamental complexes, the mother complex and the father complex." [22]

---

[21] J. Jacobi, The Psychology of C.G. Jung, p. 36.
[22] Dieckmann, *Complexes,* p. 3.

Jung explained that complexes have an archetypal core, meaning that the central image of the complex can be related to an archetype.[23] Therefore, the mother and father complexes can be related to the Mother and Father archetypes, and so to the Nature archetype through the Great Mother and Great Father archetypes that are personifications of nature. A representation of the development of the feminine archetype, based on Jacobi's description, is shown in Figure 2. The feminine archetype has been used to form an image of nature based on the work by Erich Neumann (Figure 3). The development of the masculine archetype would similarly portray the Great Father, or positive and negative personifications of the masculine in human mythic history.

We refer to complexes in modern life as "hot buttons" or "triggers," even though these triggers are actually the things that activate our complexes, and not the complexes themselves, which are unconscious. On a collective level the words *hazardous waste, toxic chemicals*, *environmental contamination*, and *pollution* are all trigger words that constellate a complex. For example, the permitting process to build a hazardous waste incinerator in a neighborhood will trigger a collective complex and a community will turn out en masse to public hearings.

There are many basic survival components clustered in this group reaction, including safety and health, reproduction, property values and environmental degradation. At the core of this cluster of complexes is the Nature archetype because these words stimulate images related to the shadowy destructive and terrible side of nature. A complex may also contain the shadow—"the sum of those personal characteristics that the individual wishes to hide from others and from himself."[24] comprised of images or issues we choose to ignore or that are distasteful to us because they stimulate fears of personal harm such as famine, cancer and death.

Essentially, hazardous chemicals and toxic substances can hide in nature and are therefore insidious, invisible and uncontrollable. We do not like the feelings that these words stimulate in us because they remind us of our vulnerability, frailty and dependence on nature. They force us to confront the cycles of human life.

---

23 Jacobi, The Psychology of C. G. Jung, p. 39.
24 Henri Ellenberger, The Discovery of the Unconscious, p. 707.

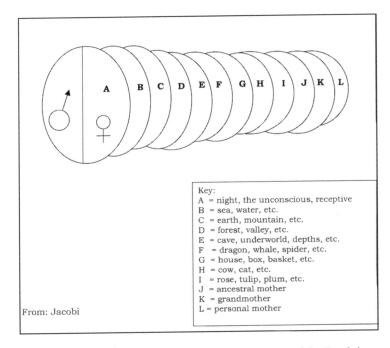

Figure 2. Developmental Sequence of the Archetype of the Feminine.

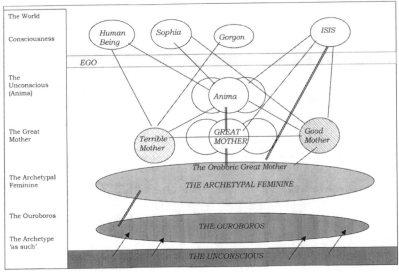

Figure 3. The Archetypal Feminine and the Great Mother.

Archetypes

Jung developed his theories on archetypes between 1912 and 1958. Over this time, his definitions of an archetype expanded as he incorporated his thoughts on issues such as myth and alchemy. Initially, Jung observed universal patterns in human cultures and myths through history. As a biological scientist, he reported instinctual patterns related to humans as instinctual creatures. As a psychologist, he observed that religions and religious traditions, cultural stories, rituals and myths show repeating patterns and images. He called these patterns in the human psyche archetypes, based on a previous definition he attributed to St. Augustine.[25] Jung saw archetypes as components of the collective unconscious, and noted that they served to organize, inform and direct human thought and behavior.

In the passage quoted at the beginning of this chapter, Jung describes archetypes as systems of readiness for action. He first noted them as "primordial images"[26] and later observed that "archetypes present themselves as ideas and images, like everything else that becomes a content of consciousness."[27] His patients' images sometimes included recurring cultural motifs of which they had no previous knowledge. Jung wrote of a case where a man observed a phallus on the sun (a "solar phallus"), a motif associated with a religious cult of which the patient knew nothing.[28] Thus Jung stated that archetypal images are numinous, unconscious and autonomous:

> In every individual, in addition to the personal memories there are also, in Jacob Burckhardt's excellent phrase, the great "primordial images", the inherited potentialities of human imagination. . . . This inheritance explains . . . that the matter of themes of certain legends are met with all the world over in identical forms.[29]

---

[25] "Instinct and the Unconscious," *The Structure and Dynamics of the Psyche*, CW 8, par. 275.

[26] "On the Relation of Analytical Psychology to Poetry," *The Spirit in Man, Art, and Literature*, CW 15, par. 127.

[27] "On the Nature of the Psyche," *The Structure and Dynamics of the Psyche*, CW 8, par. 435.

[28] "The Song of the Moth," *Symbols of Transformation*, CW 5, par. 151.

[29] "Psychology of Unconscious Processes," *Collected Papers*, p. 410.

Jung also used the terms "non-personal dominants," "archetypes of apperception," "engrams,"[30] and "collective representations"[31] before he came to "archetypes as such" and "archetypal images."[32]

Jung used a number of examples when trying to explain this concept. Using a chemical analogy, he states:

> The archetype might perhaps be compared to the axial system of a crystal, which, as it were, preforms the crystalline structure in the mother liquid, although it has no material existence of its own. This first appears according to the specific way in which the ions and molecules aggregate. . . . The axial system determines only the stereometric structure but not the concrete form of the individual crystal.[33]

Using Jung's crystal analogy as a model for the Nature archetype, the mother liquor for a crystal could be the unconscious fusion of early humanity in the world of nature. The crystalline structure thus formed would be humanity's first consciousness that grows into the crystals of civilization. The image of the crystal corresponds to the diverse nature of human towns and cities throughout the world that are shaped by the local environments of soil, geology, hydrology, biology, culture, and religion.

In 1934, Jung revised his description of the archetype to differentiate the "archetype as such" from the "archetypal image" with the term "collective representations," emphasizing the idea that things have an archetypal quality as their common denominator. He explained further:

> An archetypal content expresses itself, first and foremost, in metaphors. If such content should speak of the sun and identify with it the lion, the king, the hoard of gold guarded by the dragon, or the power that makes for the life and health of man, it is neither the one thing nor the other, but the unknown third thing that finds more or less adequate expression in all these similes, yet—to the perpetual vexation of the intellect—remains unknown and not to be fitted into a formula.[34]

---

30 "The Type Problem in Poetry," *Psychological Types,* CW 6, par. 281.

31 "Definitions," ibid., par. 692.

32 "On the Natureof the Psyche," *The Structure and Dynamics of the Psyche,* CW 8, par. 417.

33 "Psychological Aspects of the Mother Archetype," *The Archetypes and the Collective Unconscious,* CW 9i, par.155.

34 "The Psychology of the Child Archetype," ibid., par. 267.

This aspect of the Nature archetype is seen in the multitude of names given to it, such as Mother earth, Gaia, Pacha-mama, etc., where these names are more than simply names for the earth in other languages, they imply facets of life and hold spiritual meaning.

Jung's comments on archetypes relative to human instinctual behavior are also important when considering the Nature archetype because nature, the animal kingdom in particular, is driven by an involuntary need for food, water, shelter and reproduction. In Freudian terms, humans are driven by sex and aggression, both of which are expressions of our animal instinctual nature.

Jung noted that "too much of the animal distorts the civilized man, too much civilization makes sick animals,"[35] and that "instincts in their original strength can render social adaptation almost impossible."[36]

Archetypes are not solely biological instincts. Instead, Jung imagined that archetypes have instinctual and spiritual poles, similar to the light spectrum. The infrared end of the spectrum represents the dynamism of instinct and connects with the body.[37] The other end of the spectrum, the spiritual, or paradoxical quality of the archetype, is on the ultraviolet end. As indicated in Figure 1, Jung considered that each archetype is connected to the collective unconscious. He argued that there is a relationship between the human psyche and archetypes through a hypothetical medium he called a "psychoid layer." He also reasoned that the spiritual pole of the archetype is a "psychoid" factor and incapable of reaching consciousness.[38] However, Jung argued that the instinctual pole of the archetype is rooted in the body and is enlivened through bodily experience, that is, there is a mind-body connection.

In relation to the Nature archetype, one experiences nature as a physical phenomenon through our environment (trees, rivers, mountains, etc). In a psychological sense, one experiences the Nature archetype through our feelings about the intense physical drives in our bodies (hormonal

---

[35] "The Eros Theory," *Two Essays on Analytical Psychology,* CW 7, par. 32.
[36] "The Transcendent Function," *The Structure and Dynamics of the Psyche,* CW 8, par. 161.
[37] "On the Nature of the Psyche," ibid., par. 414.
[38] Ibid., par. 417.

urges, hunger, love, and fear of the power of nature). Our psychological connection to the Nature archetype is also felt in our numinous experiences of nature. It can result in an upwelling in our body and mind that feels like a spiritually transforming essence. It fuels our soul like an experience of the Self, or what might be called the presence of God, or the Divine. When the Peruvian shamans connect with Pacha-mama, their Great Mother, they do it through a felt-sense in their bodies that joins them to the holy mountain of their ancestors.[39]

The Nature Archetype As Great Mother

In his book, *The Great Mother,* Erich Neumann discusses the archetypal origins of the Mother archetype and its connection to nature through the Goddess religions. Figure 3 shows how Neumann represents the Great Mother archetype, and how it is projected into the world in the form of personified Goddess deities such as Sophia and Isis. This figure shows that humanity is connected to both the good Mother and the terrible aspects of the personified Mother archetype.

In Neumann's work, Sophia is the "gracious" Mother who pours forth her riches;[40] she symbolizes the spiritualized aspect of nature. In the Gnostic tradition, Sophia represents wisdom and a universal consciousness, and it is the goal of humanity to redeem Sophia from being trapped in matter.[41] This can be seen as a metaphor for liberating our spiritual relationship with nature from our concrete dependence on the earth as a source of material goods.

On a conscious level, if we cannot recognize the spirit in nature as important we will find it difficult to be in relationship with nature and ultimately protect it, not for esoteric or religious reasons, but as a practical matter; nature is where we live. Jung states, "No penal code and no moral code, not even the sublimest casuistry, will ever be able to codify and pronounce just judgment upon the confusions, the conflict of duty, and the invisible tragedies of the natural man in collision with the exigencies of culture. 'Spirit,' is one aspect, 'Nature' another. 'You may

---

39 Inge Bolin, *Rituals of Respect,* p. 32.
40 The Great Mother, p. 15.
41 Violet MacDermot, *The Fall of Sophia,* p. 31

pitch Nature out with a fork, yet she'll always come back again," say the poets."[42] In other words, not even legal judgments will bring clarity to the ways in which we impact nature.

Also in Neumann's work, Isis represents that aspect of the Great Mother who brings him back to life (as with Horus, who is stung by a scorpion) or who suckles the helpless child, or saves the child from the devouring father.[43]

However, the personification of nature as only a Great Mother is a one-sided representation of the Nature archetype, as is the idea that nature is controlled by a single dualistic, benevolent and vengeful Judeo-Christian masculine God. Nature has both masculine and feminine qualities in equal parts, and the Nature archetype should be viewed as having both aspects fully present. As psychological factors, one aspect or the other can be relegated to the unconscious (or shadow), fostering the idea that nature is one sided. Since earth as mother provides, much as a mother provides for an infant, I will continue the discussion from this perspective.

Return to Nature

The Great Mother is a common personification of nature because we are fed by nature. Within the last few hundred years, the feminine aspects of the Nature archetype are found in the idea of the *anima mundi,* or World Soul. The *anima mundi* is the soul of the earth (the planet) into which spirit flows. Jung referred to the alchemists on the subject:

> The spirit "that penetrates all things," or shapes all things, is the World Soul: The soul of the world therefore is a certain only thing, filling all things, bestowing all things binding and knitting together all things that it might make one frame of the world.[44]

However, I believe that when Jung discusses "the spirit that penetrates all things," he is also referring to the Nature archetype, or an aspect of the Self. James Hillman argues that the World Soul permeates all things, and

---

[42] The Great Mother, p. 43.

[43] Ibid.

[44] "Synchronicity: An Acausal Connecting Principle," *The Structure and Dynamics of the Psyche,* CW 8, par. 931.

even the city has nature's beauty because "cities belong to human nature." He states:

> Then Anima Mundi indicates the animated possibility presented by each event as it is, its sensuous presentation as a face bespeaks its interior image—in short, its availability to imagination, its presence as a psychic reality.[45]

The idea of the earth as "feminine" has led to "deep ecology,"[46] which promotes the protection of the earth. However, the modern-day feminist movement criticizes this perspective because it is a masculine viewpoint from a position of male power and is detrimental to both women and the environment because women and nature become objects. Eco-feminism draws the obvious parallels that men exploit both women and nature and men deny the interdependent and relational quality necessary to approach both.[47] Similarly, Susan Rowland notes that the psychoanalytic view represents a continuation of the gendered metaphysics of nature that is conditional upon suppressing the (m)other and adopting a transcendent relationship to the unconscious (and nature) under the name "father." [48]

As stated above, the Nature archetype is not just feminine, but also has a masculine component. A diagram similar to Figure 2 could be developed as a sequence from the personal father, through the stewards of nature, such as the farmer, the shepherd, the forester, or the Green Man, and also through active natural images such as the river, volcanoes, fire, and lightning. Eastern philosophies might refer to these as *yang* energies, compared to the feminine *yin.* Both are necessary.

In Jung's writing on the human psyche and its relationship to the earth, he describes the ancient and alchemical notion of the *anima mundi,* or world soul. This is a feminine aspect of nature.[49] He speculates about

---

45 Hillman, *On the Anima Mundi* (online); see also Hillman, "The Return of the Soul of the World," in *Spring 1982,* p. 71.
46 See A. Naess and D. Rothenberg, Ecology, Community and Lifestyle: Outline of an Ecosophy.
47 Susan Griffin, *Woman and Nature: The Roaring Inside Her,* pages 5ff.
48 "Nature Writing: Jung's Eco-logic in the *Coniunctio* of Comedy and Tragedy," in *Spring 75* (2006), pp. 275ff.
49 "Synchronicity: An Acausal Connecting Principle," *The Structure and Dynamics of the Psyche,* CW 8, par. 931.

our human connection to the earth, to the *anima mundi*, through the psychoid layer of the psyche, and suggests that we are influenced by it.

The Psychoid

By 1958, Jung became interested in archetypes and the psychoid process, which he discussed as the psychoid archetype:

> Psyche is essentially conflict between blind instinct and will (freedom of choice). Where instinct predominates, *psychoid* processes set in which pertain to the sphere of the unconscious as elements incapable of consciousness. The psychoid process is not the unconscious as such, for this has a far greater extension.[50]

Further, Jung theorized that our personal unconscious is connected through a psychoid process to the collective unconscious (see Figure 1). It is through this deep connection to the collective unconscious that Jung's theory of synchronicity works. Jung believed the wisdom gained through synchronicity was far beyond that of our conscious knowledge. He postulates that there is a place in which the inner and the outer worlds of psyche and matter are connected in an undifferentiated unity. In the Middle Ages, this unified-feeling world was called the *unus mundus*.

Jung and the physicist Wolfgang Pauli looked for evidence of this world, and theorized that a unified psychophysical reality exists beyond the split in matter and psyche.[51] The concept of *unus mundus* is important when discussing the Nature archetype because it represents the notion of a unified field of energy through which the human psyche is in contact with the Nature archetype, and so with nature. We feel its presence in our body. Jerome Bernstein proposes that certain individuals are extra sensitive to non-rational phenomena in the natural universe.[52] He has described individuals with "borderline consciousness," discussing their particularly intense and "sacred" relationship with nature. Many of these individuals feel damage to the environment in their own physical bodies, and are very sensitive to environmental change.

---

[50] "On the Nature of the Psyche," ibid., par. 380.
[51] See C. A. Meier, *Atom and Archetype: The Pauli/Jung Letters,* 1932-1958, and J. Gary Sparks, *At the Heart of Matter: Synchronicity and Jung's Spiritual Testament.*
[52] Bernstein, *Living in the Borderline,* p. 91.

Shadow

"The shadow is the sum of those personal characteristics that the individual wishes to hide from the other and from himself."[53] It represents a place in the unconscious where we put those things we find distasteful about ourselves or that we would find painful if we were to claim them. Jung distinguished between two types of shadow, personal and collective. Our personal shadow contains those traits we do not like, or we are unable to see and accept in ourselves; we often project them onto other people. The collective shadow functions in a similar way for the group. The projection of collective shadow can result in conflict or wars between countries or ethnic and religious groups.

Where nature is concerned, the collective shadow is important because it represents those areas where we are blind to our own behavior as a society. Clearly, the release of greenhouse gases and hazardous wastes without regard for the consequences arises from the collective environmental shadow. There are many who deny that these emissions are affecting the world and that we need to change our behavior. Also, there is a danger of projecting our collective environmental shadow onto developing countries. The United States is one of the greatest polluters in the world, yet to date has refused to ratify the Kyoto Accord. By doing so, the U.S. would admit that the developed world bears some responsibility and should demonstrate progress toward a solution. The U.S. also exports industry to the third world where labor is cheaper and environmental regulations are less restrictive, all the while keeping the homeland "clean." This is a convenient way for corporations to avoid dealing with the legislation and regulations of emissions and cleanup. Psychologically, it is a concretization of projected shadow. As Jung notes, "then it soon becomes apparent that the shadow has not dissolved into nothing but is only waiting for a favourable opportunity to reappear as a projection upon one's neighbour."[54]

In individual Jungian psychoanalysis, one is first required to work on one's personal shadow and issues that arise surrounding it. The shadow

---

[53] Henri Ellenberger, The Discovery of the Unconscious, p. 707.
[54] "On the Psychology of the Trickster-Figure," *The Archetypes and the Collective Unconscious,* CW 9i, par. 477.

is also where one finds creative innovation and ignored possibilities that can ultimately lead to new solutions. Giving value to shadow work and processing our personal shadow allows an individual to understand powerful unconscious complexes and develop a relationship with the unconscious that is transformative. This initial phase of the psychotherapeutic process allows for a more balanced view of our world.

By recognizing our personal connection to nature and environmental issues, individuals can begin to work on them consciously. On a collective level, recognizing our personal environmental shadow is an essential starting point. Any shadow work will help humanity to recognize the collective shadow represented by the dumping of toxins and wastes into the environment, and give value to a relationship with nature (instead of domination over it). Transformation, or at least an opportunity for change, might occur on a collective level as a result.

Nature As a Complete Biological System

With this idea of shadow in mind, it is important to look at the "biological model" of nature as other in order to gain psychological insight into our relationship with it. Theodore Roszak proposed that "the whole of the cosmos is a single great organism."[55] Ecopsychologists are animistic; that is, they believe that animals, plants and rocks have souls or spirits, and that animism is an earlier, wiser stage of development.[56] However, I don't believe we can go backward in consciousness. In his ideas on ecopsychology, Roszak draws on the work of Gaia theorists.

In 1974, Lovelock and Margulis[57] published their thoughts on Gaia, a name for the earth as a biological system that evokes an image of the Great Mother from Greek mythology. Gaia is a way to think of the earth as a single self-balancing organism in space.[58] Gaia theory promotes the view that life is a planetary scale phenomenon that sufficient living organisms are necessary for regulation of the environment, that the growth

---

[55] Roszak, *The Voice of the Earth: An Exploration of Ecopsychology,* p. 139.

[56] See J. Mach, *Inventing a Psychology of Our Relationship with the Earth.* See also www.ecopsychology.org.

[57] See J. E. Lovelock and L. Margulis, "Atmospheric Homeostasis by and for the Biosphere—The Gaia Hypothesis," in *Tellus 26* (1), pp. 2ff.

[58] J. Lovelock, *The Age of Gaia,* p. 19.

of an organism affects the physical and chemical environment, and that increased diversity of species leads to better regulation.[59] In a later book, Lovelock provides more information on Gaia, suggesting that unless renewable and sustainable forms of energy are used, the climate crisis on the earth will increase.[60]

If we hypothesize that the earth is a unified biological system like a single cell, we could then consider how such an organism behaves. Its nourishment is provided by the sun, which is converted to usable and transportable energy by parts of the cell (trees, grasses, algae and bacteria). The energy converted by these species is taken in and consumed by others (animals, fish, birds). All cells make byproducts that are either excreted or converted and stored in a form that does not harm the cell. When waste products build up in a cell their production is controlled by biological processes, including inhibitory feedback mechanisms that stop biological reactions from moving forward if they are detrimental to the life of the organism and can kill it. The analogy for the earth is obvious: if waste and heat build up on the earth, they will potentially lead to localized health problems, environmental problems, or even drastic global changes.

A single cell is like an island within defined borders. The first response to the accumulation of byproducts within a cell is for the operations that make waste to slow down or stop. These responses operate through a feedback mechanism. If we consider the earth in the same way as we view the structure of the cell, we can see where food shortages cause starvation and in turn reduce the population. From nature's perspective, overpopulation and overcrowding may be one of the Nature archetype's mechanisms of directing or managing behavior. If humanity is unable to manage itself, starvation has proven an effective method by which nature limits population growth where only the stronger and healthier members survive to reproduce. Though the human ego may consider these harsh feedback mechanisms, nature's goal is survival and such events can serve to raise humanity's collective consciousness. However, increased consciousness can only arise if we are attuned to the

---

59 Ibid., p. 63.
60 See Lovelock,"State of the Earth," in *The Revenge of Gaia,* pp. 1ff.

problem and can reflect on nature's suggestions for solutions. This requires a flexible solid ego capable of doing inner work.

Briefly returning to Jung's archetypal view that is relevant here, he states:

> The reason our consciousness exists, and why there is an urge to widen and deepen it, is very simple: without consciousness things go less well. This is obviously the reason why Mother Nature deigned to produce consciousness, that most remarkable of all nature's curiosities. Even the well-nigh primitive can adapt and assert himself, but he falls victim to countless dangers which we on a higher level of consciousness can avoid without effort. True, a higher consciousness is exposed to dangers undreamt of by the primitive, but the fact remains that the conscious man has conquered the earth and not the unconscious one. Whether in the last analysis, and from a superhuman point of view, this is an advantage or a calamity, we are not in a position to decide.[61]

One poignant example is Easter Island, which was once a thriving forest and now is relatively barren. The native population cut down the trees and used them to transport and erect the famous faces of their gods found there today. Seed and sapling loss due to rats brought by settlers prevented regrowth. Deforestation led to soil erosion, which led to poor agriculture and eventually starvation that led to a limited and poorly nourished population. The inhabitants knew the loss of the trees was detrimental to their existence, and nature's feedback mechanism eventually limited their ability to survive. Poor agriculture now limits the size of the population that can be sustained.[62]

The big question is why the inhabitants continued to cut down trees when they knew it would diminish their lives. It appears, from the archeological case study, that they were gripped by an "ideological pathology," followed by clan warfare that continued in a self-contained way until the outside world, in the form of the explorer Cook, came to the island. The archeologists said the islanders:

> carried out for us the experiment of permitting unrestricted population

---

61 "Analytical Psychology and 'Weltanschauung'," *The Structure and Dynamics of the Psyche*, CW 8, par. 695.
62 See R. Wright, A Short History of Progress, pp. 59ff.

growth, profligate use of resources, destruction of the environment and boundless confidence in their religion to take care of the future. The result was an ecological disaster leading to a population crash. . . . Do we have to repeat the experiment on [a] grand scale? Is the human personality always the same as that of the person who felled the last tree?[63]

Image of the Nature Archetype

I see the Nature archetype as a universal life principal with a psychological manifestation that is in relationship with the physical world. We are surrounded by nature and images of it. Figure 4 is my attempt to represent the Nature archetype similar to Neumann's (Figure 3). The Nature archetype is an aspect of the Self, the *Imago Dei,* and so is part of the mystery of our unconscious. However, from a temporal perspective the Nature archetype was present in the psyche before humanity became conscious of being separate from nature while still within it. It is therefore pictured in Figure 4 as being present inside the human psyche. The Nature archetype could be imaged as welling up from the collective unconscious into consciousness in the human psyche.

The right side of the diagram shows the manifestations of the physical universe including plants, animals, earth, rivers, sea, planets, suns, galaxies, etc.

From a psychological perspective, early humanity was merged with nature in a state of *participation mystique*, an unconscious fusion. Eventually, consciousness emerged in the presence of, or through the actions of, the Nature archetype, as discussed later. The left side of the diagram shows this development of consciousness starting with *participation mystique*. As consciousness developed, aspects of the Nature archetype became personified as nature gods and goddesses. Examples of the environment gods in this diagram would be Gaia, Demeter, Dionysus, the Green Man and chthonic spirits. By extension, the Nature archetype can also be seen as personified aspects of the masculine and feminine in the unconscious, the *anima*[64] and *animus*.[65]

---

63 Ibid., p. 63.
64 "Archetypes of the Collective Unconscious," *The Archetypes and the Collective Unconscious,* CW 9i, par. 66.
65 See *Aion,* CW 9ii, par. 28, and *Two Essays,* CW 7, par. 336.

The diagram shows that when the Nature archetype is expressed in the conscious world, instinctual needs rise as either shadow behavior (over extraction of resources) or its opposite (conservation). The concept of the Nature archetype is analogous to that of an atom's electron, which is pictured by scientists as either a particle or a wave, but not both at the same time.[66] The Nature archetype can be seen as the concrete aspects of nature, with instinctual drives and physical desires. It can also be seen as psychological energy that exerts pressure over time and space to influence consciousness.

In his writings on civilization, Jung describes how non-technological societies have a strong relationship to nature and the spiritual aspects of the earth where the environment is held in high regard.[67] These societies can be seen as containing both the instinctual and spiritual poles of the Nature archetype. Jung also describes how the Church and science have served to systemically demystify and de-deify our earlier relationship to nature. Relatively primitive societies also have a more direct relationship with plants and animals that keeps them closer to life and death.

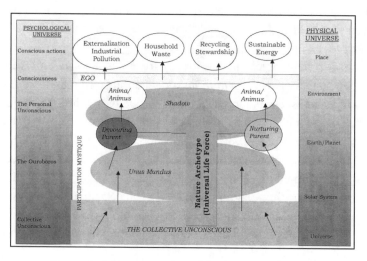

Figure 4. A Representation of the Nature archetype.

---

[66] Serdyuk et al., Methods in Molecular Biophysics, p. 887.
[67] "Archaic Man," *Civilization in Transition,* par. 128.

In 1996, while investigating an oil spill on Indian land in Montana, I spent a week with a member of the Kootenai tribe on the Flathead Indian Reservation. We discussed native hunting rituals and his preparations for the hunt. He shared stories of how the hunter honors the "sacrifice" that the animal makes. The game was overhunted and scarce, yet he held the belief that game was still present in the woods; they simply refused to be seen and to sacrifice themselves to the hunter.

In today's American society our spiritual connection to nature's sacrifice has been severed. We no longer hunt for food to survive and if we do hunt, it is typically for sport. Many of us no longer know where our food comes from or the process it goes through to arrive at our tables. If people had to kill, gut and pluck a chicken before their Sunday roast or barbeque, I wonder how many would eat less meat. Instead of a direct relationship with crops and game that constellates the spiritual pole of the Nature archetype, it seems as if modern society's connection depends upon individual value sets expressed through driving a hybrid car, living off the grid, buying eco-friendly stocks, or advocating for nature in the community. This connection might also be constellated through a nature-oriented spiritual practice. All these expressions of the spiritual pole of the Nature archetype are influenced by the Self and involve making a sacrifice in recognition of our place in nature.

Since the April 2010 release of oil from the BP/Trans-oceanic well, a large area of the Gulf has been polluted. Large fishing and shrimping areas in the region have been destroyed or contaminated. The Gulf provided a third of the U.S. oyster and shrimp crops from the waters along the Louisiana coast.[68] It is only when a disaster of the magnitude of this spill occurs that we see our complex dependence on nature. In one way, the fishing townsfolk of Louisianan and Alabama now share a common bond, a trauma bond, with the native tribes of Montana and of Prince William Sound. Their native food species have been sacrificed for a modern way of life.

The following chapter presents a few myths showing how humanity has interacted with nature in the past, and the result of these interactions.

---

68 Bruce Barcott, "Forlorn in the Bayou," in *National Geographic,* October 2010, pp. 62ff.

3
Creation and Nature Mythology

Myths are therefore like reflections or a mirroring of certain cultural situations of mankind, and like great, archetypal individual dreams, they contain deep intuitions and anticipations of further developments, and thus they can be considered as milestones in the development of human consciousness.[69]

It is impossible to talk about the Nature archetype without discussing creation mythology because creation myths are about "the origins of man's conscious awareness of the world."[70] Humanity developed self-awareness or consciousness in relation to an "Other." Early in our history, the Other was nature. It is the place where we become self-aware, for example, in the arms of the m(other). Consequently, there is a great deal of creation mythology related to nature. As Marie-Louise von Franz notes, myths indicate that humanity found a way to conceptualize a psychological beginning, where we first perceived ourselves as separate from nature. From being in *participation mystique* with our environment, we developed into a state of separateness, then began to realize our vulnerability to the power of nature and sought to gain dominion over it. Jung writes:

> In the course of its ontogenetic development, the individual ego consciousness has to pass through the same archetypal stages which determined the evolution of consciousness in the life of humanity.[71]

Jung is suggesting that psychologically we repeat patterns of human cultural development in our individual biological development. Therefore, our separation from what Jung calls an Ouroboric state (unconsciousness) in nature is equivalent to the separation from our personal mother. Erich Neumann too described the process from a Jungian per-

---

[69] R. S. Kluger, *The Archetypal Significance of Gilgamesh*, p. 17.
[70] Von Franz, *Creation Myths*, p. 8.
[71] *Symbols of Transformation*, CW 5, par. 26.

spective, observing that separation from nature and separation from the personal mother are the initial steps in humanity's conscious development.[72]

Creation and Feminine Archetypal Patterns

Neumann identified feminine religions as an archetypal pattern in world creation mythology. The created world is endowed with female qualities that reflect her fecund nature; that is, she has the ability to produce and feed life in seemingly endless ways. Like an infant child, early humanity once saw itself at the center and her abundance as their support.

The Greek myth of Gaia is important to the discussion of nature for a number of reasons. Gaia was the original mother who provided for humanity. As mentioned earlier in Chapter Two, Lovelock draws on this myth to name the concept of earth as a single biological system.

Greek Creation Myth—Chaos and Gaia

In one of the most well-known Greek creation myths, Hesiod attributes the rank of senior goddess to Gaia, the Earth. Ouranos, the sky god, comes at night to impregnate Gaia and she gives him children. He does not like his offspring and, in his cruelty, he hides them inside the Earth (inside her). According to the myth, Gaia feels afflicted by the rejection of her creations. She therefore brings forth iron and makes a sickle. She talks with her children, and her son Kronos says he will deal with their father. He takes the sickle and castrates Ouranos, casting his genitalia into the sea. Out of the blood and wounding are born the Erinyes (the Furies), Giants and the Ash Nymphs. And from the genitals, the love goddess Aphrodite is born.

After this, sky and earth are severed from each other, never to come together again. This act and the subsequent separation suggest a limit on procreation. The children of Earth and Sky, Rhea and Kronos, marry and have three daughters and three sons. A war between the family of the father (the Titans) and the family of the son (the Olympians) ensues. Eventually the Titans are defeated and Zeus becomes the ruler of Mount Olympus and the Greek pantheon of gods. A masculine god rules over

---

72 Neumann, *The Origins and History of Consciousness*, p. 43.

humanity's activities from the heavens, a position above the earth and separate from it.

Perhaps it is from this position that we, too, see and engage with nature. Although the feminine goddesses have a place in the Greek pantheon of gods, they do not rule, and although respect remains for Gaia's help in defeating the Titans, she becomes part of the old pantheon that is displaced. The feminine goddess Demeter is then seen as the goddess of the fruits of the earth. However, even she is subject to the excesses of the masculine. Demeter has a daughter Persephone. In the myth, Hades, god of the underworld, abducts the virgin Persephone (the Kore) into his realm after he receives permission to do so from his brother Zeus. Persephone is held as his wife and queen. As Demeter mourns the loss of her daughter, the earth is in perpetual winter. It is not until her daughter is returned to her, at least for part of the year, that spring returns to the earth.

This myth is not only a metaphor for nature's solar cycle where a cold, desolate winter yields into spring, it is also a metaphor for our modern world as it deals with the pattern of natural disasters. Rather than being caught in the cold ice of winter, the United States seems to be caught in the seasonal hurricanes that wash in from the coast of Africa and bring destructive floods to the southern and eastern coasts. As global climate change continues to increase summer temperatures in Africa and the Atlantic Ocean, scientists predict that hurricanes will intensify, bringing more floods and greater destruction. From the perspective of what Jung called the "primitive mind," it is as if these hurricanes bring a just retribution. Scientifically, the excessive externalization of greenhouse gases is increasing the average temperature of the earth's oceans and causing hurricanes of greater intensity.

Paradoxically, natural disasters reconnect us with nature in a psychological way. If we are present during a hurricane, flood or tornado, we actually feel the force of nature and its awesome destructive strength. We feel helpless, powerless and unsafe. Hurricanes also symbolize the Self in their overwhelming connections to nature and the unconscious.[73] Such experiences reinforce our desire to control or defend against the power of

---

[73] See David Schoen, Divine Tempest: The Hurricane as a Psychic Phenomenon, p. 10.

nature. Beyond the immediate experience of it, modern society also emphasizes nature's force through television and film. Hurricanes Katrina and Gustav destroyed large sections of New Orleans and the American South while images of this destruction played over and over again on television newscasts. While the increased force of the hurricanes have been linked to global climate change, replaying these pictures helps to reiterate that hurricanes are a response by nature that threatens our safety, and they reinforce the realization that we are powerless in the face of nature's might.

Norse Creation Myth—The World Tree and Ragnarok

The violence and destructive force of natural disasters suggests the myth of Ragnarok, which comes at the end of the Norse creation myth cycle. Snorri Snurluson wrote *The Prose Edda* around 1220, telling of how the Norse world was created from fire and ice.[74]

The first ice giants were born from the sweat of the evil frost giant Ymir, who was sleeping on the ice. As more primordial ice melted, the liquid took the form of a cow, Audumla, who fed off the ice and produced milk that nourished the developing world.[75] The cow is another symbol of the great mother, and represents fecundity. Audumla continued to lick the ice and eventually uncovered a man, Buri. His son Bor married the daughter of the ice giants, Bestela, and their three sons Odin, Villi and Ve killed the evil Ymir and used his body to create the world. These brothers created man and woman from the wood of ash and elm trees. The Norse pantheon of gods is more balanced than the Greek, with twelve men and twelve women, and is more closely linked to nature and its cycles.

Central to the creation of the world of Norse mythology was the world tree, Yggdrasil, whose roots penetrated all levels of the world. The tree is an important image in mythology, in the development of human society and in the environment. Jung sees the tree as an image of the mother[76]

---

74 Snurluson, *The Prose Edda,* p. x.
75 K. Crossly-Holland, *The Norse Myths,* p. 4.
76 "Symbols of the Mother and of Rebirth," *Symbols of Transformation,* CW 5, pars. 348ff.

and the Great Mother.[77]

In both the Greek and Norse mythologies, there is a battle between the chthonic elements represented by the giants and the seeming more progressive winners of the battles. From a psychological perspective, banishing or relegating the chthonic aspects of our selves to an inferior position, or the unconscious, is symbolic of dominating nature.

The end of the Norse myth culminates with Ragnarok, an epic battle between the giants and the Aesir, as the Norse Gods called themselves. After the battle, Baldur, the Norse god of light and purity, is reborn to a field of green. In nature symbolism this would represent the return of the sun, or Spring. And from a psychological perspective, Baldur symbolizes consciousness. This image, Ragnarok and the rebirth of Baldur, may also be symbolic. Consciousness is gained only after a battle where the tension of opposites is neutralized, or there is environmental destruction and a rebirth of nature-consciousness.

Dominance over Nature

In humanity's early development, nature is represented by the feminine. The next step in development shows how the masculine establishes dominance over her. Two myths illustrate this early relationship between humanity and nature: the Sumerian myth of Gilgamesh and the Greek myth of Erysichthon. These myths are early records of humanity's propensity (call it an archetypal pattern) to overuse and abuse nature.

Gilgamesh and Enkidu

Gilgamesh was an historical king of Uruk in Babylonia, on the River Euphrates in modern Iraq; he lived about 2700 B.C. Many stories and myths about Gilgamesh were written down about 2000 B.C. on clay tablets that still survive

The civilization of the Tigris-Euphrates area was among the first known civilizations. The myth of Gilgamesh is significant in humanity's relationship with nature because it reflects the battle of the masculine "hero" over the feminine earth goddesses and represents the incorporation of agriculture into civilization. There are two particular aspects of

---

[77] "The Archetype in Dream Symbolism," *The Symbolic Life,* CW 18, par. 550.

the Gilgamesh myth that are relevant here: the felling of the cedars of Lebanon and the killing of the Bull of Heaven.

In the myth, Gilgamesh is an arrogant human king who is also part god. No one can stop him from taking brides from their husbands on the first night of their marriage. His sexual appetite seems insatiable. To help subdue him, the sacred prostitutes of Ishtar's temple find a wild man (Enkidu, who lives with the animals) and seduce him into civilization. Enkidu is brought into the city and will not submit to Gilgamesh, so the two fight. The battle is fierce and Gilgamesh finally wins. Through the experience, the two become inseparable friends. They then embark on a quest to fell the great cedars of Lebanon.

When Gilgamesh and Enkidu cut down the cedars of Lebanon and kill their guardian Humbaba, it is a direct challenge to the goddess Ishtar, the forest deity. (There are parallels here with the Greek myth of Erysichthon discussed later.)

> Gilgamesh took the axe in his hand
> And cut down the cedar.
> But when Humbaba heard the noise,
> He became enraged and said, "Who has come
> And disturbed the trees that have grown up on my mountains,
> And has cut down the cedars?"[78]

Ishtar is a fertility goddess who feeds humanity, but she does not respect the masculine. Later Ishtar attempts to seduce Gilgamesh. He rejects her by describing how she takes lovers and later turns them into animals and humiliates or kills them. As the Great Mother, Ishtar can be terrible and destroying (see Figure 3), and Gilgamesh recognizes this in her. This aspect of Ishtar suggests that she allows her lovers to encounter the animal instinctual nature within themselves.[79] The myth goes on to depict many images that include Gilgamesh and Enkidu as symbols of instinctual masculine nature. This theme is also seen in the myth of Dionysus (discussed later), where the Bacchae, women in an ecstatic frenzy, put men in touch with their instinctual selves.

---

78 Alexander Heidel, The Gilgamesh Epic and Old Testament Parallels, p. 48.
79 Paul Kluger, The Archetypal Significance of Gilgamesh, p. 117.

Ishtar is enraged by Gilgamesh's rejection and sends the Bull of Heaven to Uruk, the capital city where he lives, to kill him. In the ensuing battle the Bull is killed, after which Ishtar climbs on the walls of Uruk and curses Gilgamesh:

> Woe unto Gilgamesh, who has besmirched me and has killed
>   the bull of heaven!
> When Enkidu heard this speech of Ishtar,
> He tore out the right thigh of the bull of heaven and tossed it
>   before her, saying:
> "If only I could get hold of thee,
> I would do unto thee as unto him;
> Or I would tie his entrails to thy side!"[80]

In this scene, the two heroes challenge and defeat the goddess's champion. However, in this act of defiance, Enkidu tempts fate because Ishtar is the Mother of all life. Paul Kluger sees the Bull of Heaven as a representation of Ishtar's animus, and therefore the defeat is a wounding on many levels including the personal.[81] When the gods debate the fate of Gilgamesh and Enkidu for their crimes it is decided that Enkidu should die, in particular for the felling of the cedars, which was the greater of the two crimes. In the minds of the gods, Enkidu is the more primitive of the two men and the lesser because he has no divine part (and Gilgamesh is part god). Thus Enkidu is condemned to die.

Before the sacred prostitute seduced Enkidu into civilization, he lived in the wild as an animal. In civilization he uses his instinctual energy to fight and kill Humbaba, the monster in the forest (the unconscious) and the Bull of Heaven (the dangerous parts of nature). Despite these successes, Enkidu is no longer considered useful by the new consciousness and is sacrificed. This represents a splitting of the instinctual from the civilized individual. Psychologically, a man's instinctual nature is relegated to the shadow.

In this myth, the men sacrifice their connection to part of their instinctual nature and, in the name of the heroic quest, defeat nature in the forest of Lebanon and kill the Bull of Heaven. However, nature is an eternal

---

[80] Heidel, The Gilgamesh Epic, p. 45.
[81] Kluger, The Archetypal Significance, p. 136.

goddess and an archetypal energy that cannot be destroyed. The attitude of the two heroes is a metaphor for what underlies the inflated human belief that we could gain control over nature, which persists today.

Erysichthon

In the *Metamorphoses*, Ovid tells the myth of the king Erysichthon who enters into Cere's (Demeter's) sacred grove and cuts down her sacred tree. Erysichthon is a king who does not honor nature. He scorns the goddess and when he enters the grove with an axe to cut down the tree, the Dryads (nymphs or wood spirits associated with trees), dance and circle the tree to protect it. Erysichthon says, "This may be the only tree the goddess loves; it may be the goddess herself, no matter: its leafy crest shall touch the ground."[82] When he cuts the bark of the tree, blood gushes from the wound, "as from the neck of the bull at the sacrifice."

In Ovid's tale, the Dryads go to Demeter and beg her to punish Erysichthon for ruining her sacred grove. Demeter decides to get revenge by having the goddess Famine visit Erysichthon. Famine and Demeter are opposites and represent each other's shadow, but in the face of his sacrilege, the opposites unite. Psychologically, this suggests that greed and overuse can bring about their opposite—paucity. Famine is asked to visit Erysichthon, and she does so: "She twined her skinny arms around him, filled him with what she was, breathed into his lips, his throat, and planted hunger in his hollow veins."[83]

As hunger's breath impacts Erysichthon, he is driven to consume. He goes from feast to feast eating all he can. "Enough to feed a nation is not enough for Erysichthon's hunger. The more he wolves the more he wants."[84] His feasting leaves him penniless. Erysichthon has a daughter who lost her virginity to the god Neptune. She is worried that she will be sold into slavery and begs Neptune to save her, so he changes her into a fisherman. Her father Erysichthon finds her and she is transformed back into a girl. He sells her over and over again. In the end, his need for food is so great that, with his money gone, he feeds on his own flesh.

---

[82] R. Humphries, *Ovid: Metamorphoses,* p. 205.
[83] Ibid., p. 207.
[84] Ibid.

The Erysichthon story is set in the period of the Peloponnesian War, when wood was in high demand to build ships and the forests of Greece and the Aegean were rapidly disappearing. There are many parallels between that time in history and our current predicament. The need for wood to fuel a war is similar to our current need for oil to fuel the economy. Humanity's lust for oil, the "mother's milk" of industry and growth, consumes the world and those who produce and sell it control our lives. Former President George W. Bush told America that "we are addicted to oil." The government uses two percent (2%) of the oil consumed in the U.S. today, and of the 440,000 barrels per day used by the government, 97% is used by the Department of Defense.[85]

In the Erysichthon myth, the king holds no respect for Demeter, the goddess of nature. In his mind it is acceptable to harvest wood from any source, including places considered sacred by others. A parallel situation currently exists in the United States where environmental groups are fighting offshore oil exploration and drilling for oil in Anwar. Both of these areas have been considered two of America's last remnants of unspoiled landscapes and wildlife. And as this book is being written, BP's efforts to obtain deep-sea offshore oil have resulted in one of the largest oil spills in U.S. history. Oil is our insatiable hunger. Greed and war drive the need for new sources of oil and are behind the rush to exploit resources in the same way that the Peloponnesian War was behind the deforestation of the Aegean.

The Erysichthon myth is relevant to our overuse of nature today. For instance, Erysichthon uses an axe to cut down the tree. The axe is a symbol of humanity's ability to excavate, refine and shape iron into tools, and with these tools humanity develops civilization. Also, the axe is a symbol of our power and aggression against nature. The tree is a symbol of life and is central to many myths. The tree is typically considered feminine and the center of the world, or the *axis mundi*, around which the world is organized. In Norse mythology, the tree Yggdrasil is central to the world. The sacred *ceiba* or *yaxché* of the Yucatan Mayas grows at the center of the world and supports the layers of the sky. In each of the four regions of the world, one colored tree of this species serves as a corner-

---

85 Peak Oil, 2006 (online).

pillar for the heavens. The tree is also at the center of the Biblical Eden and symbolizes life lived in accordance with God's plan.[86]

When the sacred tree is cut down, Demeter, the goddess of fecundity, constellates her shadow of paucity or hunger. The goddess Famine infects and consumes Erysichthon and he becomes possessed. Ovid uses the image of the devouring wolf as a symbol for the ravenous instinct that cannot be satiated. At that time in Greece, a woman's humanity was devalued and she was considered nothing more than property. Psychologically, Erysichthon devalues his internal feminine (his anima-daughter) and his Self. When Erysichthon's daughter transforms into a fisherman to avoid him, he finds her and sells her over and over again. This suggests that Erysichthon is subject to a repetition compulsion that is supported by the return of his daughter each time she is sold. This repeated selling cuts Erysichthon off from the feminine and the Self, in the same way that modern patriarchal society values the search for more oil and cuts itself off from nature. In the myth, nature has her revenge through the intervention of Famine, which is also applicable today.

Many modern day industries fit psychologically with this pattern, and the most disheartening is the use of corn to make fuel for cars. I see an inherent moral problem with burning food as it runs contrary to the feminine principles of Demeter, fecundity, and the Nature archetype. Burning food threatens the economic security of the poor by driving up food prices. It could eventually cause starvation in the world. In response to the use of corn for fuel, the price of corn has increased, contributing to increased world food prices. In other words, plentiful food resources will be channeled into the production of fuel and inexpensive, sustainable sources of food will diminish. This process is often encouraged by government subsidies to agribusiness.

Hopi Creation Myth

In a Hopi creation myth, the people are made by the creator and live on one level of a multi-leveled world. They pollute and dump their wastes into the world to a point where they cannot live on that level any

---

86 H. Biedermann, Dictionary of Symbolism, Culture Icons and the Meanings Behind Them, pp. 350f.

longer. So they turn to their god and ask to be transported to another level. The creator grants their request and gives them a ladder. They climb to a higher level where they now live, remembering to honor the environment in their new world. Today this myth offers no viable practical solution for us, unless we look at it symbolically and realize that the levels of the world are in fact levels of consciousness. We are required to move to another level of nature-consciousness, where nature is given value and respected.

In a way, this myth illustrates the fact that native cultures often live closer to nature than industrial societies do; we tend to idealize their relationship with nature. In the myth the Hopi see the relationship between externalizing wastes (polluting) and the ability to live in the world. In the myth, the world is a closed system and waste does not go anywhere. Eventually, the exposure to refuse is overpowering. The myth also suggests the ease with which humanity pollutes our own consciousness. Psychologically, the story reveals a magical solution: the people ask God for help and a ladder appears to take them to another world. This trust in magical resolutions is represented today in humanity's belief that science will develop solutions to our problems. Society believes that somehow technology will invent a solution for our current environmental problems, so that we can avoid confronting the shadow of our own pollution. Even now a few respected scientists are suggesting that we could rocket wastes into the sun[87] or solve our problems by climate geoengineering.[88] Alas, such ideas would result in spreading the waste even further afield rather than reducing it.

Nature's Response

These myths illustrate how humanity came from nature and yet seeks to dominate it. However, nature is powerful. What we might call the negative or devouring mother in Jungian psychology appears and shows its force. In the following sub-sections, I provide some myths of humanity's relationship with nature. Many are helpful when considering our situation today.

---

[87] Alexei Byalko, *Nuclear Waste Disposal,* pp. 43f.
[88] Gardiner et al., *Climate Ethics,* p. 293.

56

Nemesis

Nemesis is not accounted among the twelve Olympian gods and goddesses, nor is she the goddess of nature *per se*. However, she is important
when considering nature. According to Karl Kerényi, her name means
"righteous anger."[89] This is directed against those who have violated
order, especially the order of nature, and have disregarded nature's laws
and norms. She is featured in the Callimachus *Hymn to Demeter* (Callimachus is a third-century version of the Erysichthon myth): "Erysichthon
needed timber to build a banqueting hall. An impious man, he cut down
Demeter's sacred oak grove where the nymphs were wont to dance."[90]
When one of Demeter's priestesses warns Erysichthon not to touch the
trees in Demeter's sacred grove he says,

> Vie back, lest I fix my great axe in thy flesh! These trees shall make my
> tight dwelling wherein evermore I shall hold pleasing banquets enough for
> my companions. So spake the youth and Nemesis recorded his evil
> speech.[91]

Therefore, Nemesis is very much involved in the downfall of Erysichthon through her anger at his action and her careful recording of the
event.

Psychologically, the idea of Nemesis, or just retribution, is to bring
balance to those who do not have a champion, or in this case those who
disrespect nature or put themselves above it. During the mythic Greek
era, there is a reaction to such greed and destruction, and an attempt to
understand it through stories. Today we see the greed in mineral and oil
exploration, and in logging companies—all of which have constellated
their opposites in the "Green" movement with extremist fringe eco-
terrorists. For example, eco-terrorism in Nigeria today is forcing the oil
companies and the government to address the issue of corruption. Dis-
honest politicians and government officials divert the income from huge
amounts of oil to private bank accounts rather than infusing money back
into the poor rural areas where the oil was found but currently receive no

---

[89] Kerényi, The Gods of the Greeks, p. 105.
[90] Michael Grant and John Hazel, *Who's Who in Classical Mythology,* p. 202.
[91] A. Mair, trans., Callimachus, *Hymn to Demeter,* pp. 65ff.

resource benefits. Eco-terrorists sabotage wells, hijack supply ships and rupture pipelines to force the hands of the oil companies. For instance, the radical organization called Earth First issued a manifesto stating their goal was "mutiny and sabotage in defence of Mother Earth."[92]

Embedded in the Erysichthon myth is a power complex. Erysichthon feels a personal entitlement to challenge the gods. In Nigeria, individuals within the government at one time felt so powerful that they did not respond to the needs of their own people. However, power constellates its opposite, its shadow, in the oppressed. Those who feel disenfranchised may take action to empower themselves and fight for their survival and their beliefs, going as far as eco-terrorism.

Pentheus

Another relevant psychological position is illustrated by the story of Pentheus. In the Dionysus myth a distant, intellectually dominated government ruler, Pentheus, attempts to control nature when it is in its unbridled instinctual state.

The God Zeus conceives Dionysus (Bacchus) with the mortal Semele. For conceiving the child, Zeus grants her anything she wishes. However, Hera tricks Semele into using her wish to see Zeus in his true form. When Zeus reveals himself to Semele, she is killed by a thunderbolt that incinerates her. Before Dionysus dies with his mother, Zeus snatches him up and sews him into his thigh until he is full term, whereupon he is born a second time to Zeus.[93] After this rebirth, he is immortal. In another version of the myth, Persephone is Dionysus's mother and Zeus his father. Demeter hides Persephone away in a cave guarded by serpents, but Zeus disguises himself as a serpent and copulates with her.[94] Hera is jealous and attempts to kill Dionysus by sending Titans to rip him to pieces after luring the baby with toys. Zeus drives the Titans away with his thunderbolts, but only after the Titans eat everything but his heart, which is saved by Athena (or Rhea or Demeter depending on the version of the myth) who represents the Great Mother. Zeus uses the heart to rec-

---

[92] Donald Liddick, *Eco-Terrorism,* p. 63.

[93] P. Slater, The Glory of Hera: Greek Mythology and the Greek Family, p. 230.

[94] Kerényi, Gods of the Greeks, p. 252.

reate Dionysus in the womb of Semele; hence he is again "the twice-born."

Semele is the sister of Agave who is married to Cadmus, the founder of the city of Thebes. When Cadmus is too old, he gives the city to Pentheus to rule. Pentheus and Dionysus are cousins. The story of Pentheus can also be seen as an allegory for the time of competition between different factions of Sparta and Athens (or more specifically between Cimon and Peracles). Pentheus is associated with logic and intellect, good government and prudence and is attributed to Apollo, the God of uniformity, orderliness and unadulterated seriousness.[95] In short, Pentheus represents a logos attitude.

In another way, Pentheus represents Apollo in the tension of opposites between the Dionysian and Apollonian attitudes described by Jung in his work on typology.[96] Dionysus is nature and we fear the annihilation of the individual by nature, and yet we are also drawn toward the rapturous delight in its destruction.

Each version of this myth might invoke a slightly different psychological interpretation. Yet in all the versions, Dionysus is born out of trauma and the myth originates with anger from the feminine (Hera). While Pentheus represents humanity, particularly its logical, scientific and patriarchal aspects, his cousin Dionysus symbolizes freedom of expression, passion and ecstasy. He is a masculine image of the Nature archetype. In his early life Dionysus travels widely and becomes the God of wine. He masters and teaches agriculture related to grapes, the fermentation of wine and the *Bacchae*, a ritual festival or orgy, where the participants enter into a frenzy and act without consciousness. Dionysus had a large following in many countries and gained favor with women who would participate in the ritual. He symbolizes the god of nature on a human level. For example, in one ceremony to honor Dionysus, a child is carried in a basket that was previously used to honor vegetation and the harvest. Dionysus also represents agriculture and animal fecundity, including human reproduction.

Dionysus returns to Thebes, with his followers the Maenads (meaning

---

95 P. Slater, *The Glory of Hera*, p. 230.
96 "The Apollonian and the Dionysian," *Psychological Types,* CW 6, pars. 225ff.

raging). When he returns, Semele's sisters refuse to recognize him as a God. One of Semele's sisters, Autonoe, is the mother of Aktaion who is torn to pieces by his hounds when he watches the goddess Diana bathe in the woods. Dionysus contrives the same fate for Agave, the other sister of Semele and Pentheus's mother. Except in this case, she and her sisters will be the hounds.[97] Pentheus also refuses to recognize Dionysus as a God and arrests him. Pentheus puts him in prison but his chains fall off and no jail can hold him. Dionysus convinces Pentheus to spy on the *Bacchae* and when the Maenads in their frenzy see him, he is torn apart by his mother and her sisters. The conflict between Pentheus and Dionysus reflects the conflict in attitude between the nature god and those do not have a close connection to nature. It is also a good metaphor for our current conflict between industry and nature.

If we look at this myth in relation to nature today, we see that Dionysus symbolizes the uncontrolled, emotional aspects of nature, passion and feeling. In the United States he might be the environmental activist who acts in ways that the logical collective does not understand. Julia Butterfly Hill, for example, spent 738 days in an ancient redwood tree (Luna), 180 feet above the ground to protect the thousand-year-old tree and the Headwaters Forest in which it grew.[98] To some of us her passion and perseverance were simply foolish and illogical. Others, particularly women, supported her. She felt she had a personal relationship with Luna and imagined that she could make a difference. Hill made a statement for nature by protecting the ancient symbol of nurture and as a result impacted the collective psyche.

Pentheus is also found up a tree, but in his case he is caught spying on the Dionysian rite of the Maenads. He separates himself by moving up and above, the position that is symbolically distant and represents being in one's head. Like many of today's countries and some scientists, we feel we are above nature and that we can solve problems with our logical thought processes alone. There is a lack of relationship with nature and a devaluing of it and its power. As in the myth, we feel we can put nature

---

97 Kerényi, *Gods of the Greeks,* p. 252.

98 See Julia Hill, The Legacy of Luna: The Story of a Tree, a Woman and the Struggle To Save the Redwood.

in chains, restrain her and keep her jailed. Like Dionysus, nature can loosen its chains and unleash its passion and force. However, if we could change our attitude toward nature and adopt the consciousness of Julia Hill, then, through the use of imagination, other possibilities might emerge.

The Eternal Return

Mircea Eliade, in *The Myth of the Eternal Return,* describes the role of ritual and myth in the lives of archaic humanity. The return of the sun after winter and the seasonality of life are central to early human religions and are symbolized in many creation mythologies. Through ritual, ceremony and sacrifice, the creation of the world is enacted through the archetype of repetition. Eliade states, "The creation of the world, then, is reproduced every year."[99] He also suggests that this is a rejection of linear time:

> Archaic man's rejection of history, his refusal to situate himself in a concrete, historical time, would, then be the symptom of a precocious weariness, a fear of movement and spontaneity; in short, placed between accepting the historical condition and its risks on the one hand, and his reidentification with the modes of nature on the other, he would choose such a reidentification.[100]

Eliade argues that modern humanity has rejected the archetype of repetition because it lacks creativity, and so contemporary humanity makes its own history. As a result, humanity is cut off from all creation, except things created by humanity itself. This is represented by the Biblical myth of the loss of the Garden of Eden when man ate from the tree of knowledge. Eliade states the problem for modern-day society:

> It (history) tends to be made by an increasingly smaller number of men who not only prohibit the mass of their contemporaries from directly or indirectly intervening in the history they are making (or which the small group is making), but in addition have at their disposal means sufficient to force each individual to endure, for his own part, the consequences of this history, that is to live immediately and continuously in dread of history. . .

---

[99] Eliade, The Myth of the Eternal Return. p. 62.
[100] Ibid., p. 155.

61

At most, man is left free to choose between two positions: (1) to oppose the history that is being made by the very small minority (and, in this case, he is free to choose between suicide and deportation); (2) to take refuge in a subhuman existence or in flight.[101]

From a psychological perspective, Eliade identifies two key points that are relevant here: (a) that one of the sources of humanity's anxiety is separation from nature and from the archetype of repetition (renewal); and (b) without connection to the archetype of renewal, humanity endures the anxiety of exile or death. He points out that the power complex constellates defeatist thinking and immobilizes both the individual and the collective. The archetype of renewal is also central to the Nature archetype because it is linked to the cycles of the sun and the earth.

Eliade identifies a point of departure from our mythic past and establishes the beginning of an untenable situation. According to his logic, when humanity rejects natural cycles and assumes control, we must also have the creativity to resolve the very problems we create. But the power has now moved to a few individuals, or corporations, who are not invested in changing the status quo because it would mean relinquishing power. This feels like a situation that many of us have faced when dealing with hazardous waste in our backyards, or toxic vapors coming into our houses from solvents in the groundwater or from global climate change. We are powerless to change or resolve the situation, but we are exposed to something that evokes fear and anxiety.

A regular solution is to move to a new place and be exiled from our original home, or stay and be exposed to the fear of death. This choice of "death or exile" is a double bind, where neither position is acceptable.

Although Eliade's argument is persuasive and clearly reflects the dilemma modern society faces, it does not offer much of a solution. However, Jungian psychological theory has much to offer in response to this conflict because Eliade's psychological position of "exile or death" can be viewed in a Jungian sense as a complex.

Complexes can "have us," making us feel restricted, closed off, limited and with feelings of anger and frustration, or numbness. When we

---

[101] Ibid., pp. 156f.

are in a complex we feel as if there is no resolution. Jung saw complexes as a tension between the conscious and the unconscious, and thought that by making them conscious and working with them we could expand and develop our consciousness, thus resolving the conflict. If we do this, it's almost impossible not to find fresh ways of behaving toward nature that are not regressive but rather look forward and complement our growing consciousness. The complex hinted at by Eliade (death or exile) can be resolved, at least in part, by using modern humanity's creativity and imagination to couple creative futuristic solutions with the cyclical repetition (renewal) of nature. Such solutions are to reconnect with nature through renewable energy and a solar-based society.

Eliade identifies a foundational psychological problem of the industrial era; that is, humanity has become separated from nature. This separation causes anxiety and increases our feelings of exile.

Modern humanity was first separated from a connection to nature and a sense of renewal during the Industrial Revolution. In the following chapter, I describe how I believe this came about. I personally experienced a separation from nature when I left my rural English roots, and I believe these kinds of separation experiences have increased humanity's disregard for nature. Further, I believe that this disconnection from nature has increased society's propensity to externalize our wastes onto nature, which leads to local environmental contamination and ultimately global warming.

4
Industrialization

In reality we can never legitimately cut loose from our archetypal foundations unless we are prepared to pay the price of a neurosis, any more than we can rid ourselves of our body and its organs without committing suicide. If we cannot deny the archetypes or otherwise neutralize them, we are confronted, at every new stage in the differentiation of consciousness to which civilization attains, with the task of finding a new *interpretation* appropriate to this stage, in order to connect the life of the past that still exists in us with the life of the present, which threatens to slip away from it. If this link-up does not take place a kind of rootless consciousness comes into being no longer oriented to the past, a consciousness which succumbs helplessly to all manner of suggestions, and, in practice is susceptible to psychic epidemics.[102]

I was fortunate to grow up in rural Sussex and experience a deep connection with nature. I believe it is my roots in the English countryside, in nature, that aroused my interest in local regulations, such as the laws around footpaths. In England, footpaths are open to everyone at all times; one can walk across anyone's land if it has a footpath. Under the laws, a landowner is required to keep rural footpaths open, if used. As a child, I would occasionally walk along the less used of these paths with my father to keep them open to the public. This tradition put me in touch with the land and also helped me understand the older laws. I could see value in the customs that sprang from local regulations, illustrating how nature should be available to anyone who used the footpaths.

Enclosure and the Tragedy of the Commons

I have always held an interest in local history and how village culture develops. Thus, I came to study the subject of "Enclosure."[103] This is the mechanism by which the rural English population was moved into towns

---

[102] "The Psychology of the Child Archetype," *The Archetypes of the Collective Unconscious*, CW 9i, par. 267.
[103] See J. Neeson, *Commoners: Common Right, Enclosure and Social Change.*

and cities in order to provide labor for the Industrial Revolution. As the population of rural England grew, grazing pressure on the common land, or "Commons," caused greater damage to environmental resources through overconsumption and trampling. The land became of such poor quality that it could not support the sheep and cattle and everyone suffered because of this overuse. William Forster Lloyd wrote about this [104] and it is discussed in great detail by Garrett Hardin.[105] The law of Enclosure required all common land to be fenced, thus removing access to the Commons from everyone except those to whom the land was given. The loss of grazing on common land forced poor rural families into the towns. Metaphorically, this was the sickle that cut poor English rural folk from their roots. A similar process is happening today whereby generations of U.S. young people move from the heart of rural America because there are few jobs in our current economy of megafarms and agribusinesses. Family farmers are squeezed out of business and rural families relocate to the cities.

Thucydides (ca. 460 B.C.) first identified the problem of overusing common natural resources. He expressed the concept like this:

> They devote a very small fraction of time to the consideration of any public object, most of it to the prosecution of their own objects. Meanwhile each fancies that no harm will come to his neglect, that it is the business of somebody else to look after this or that for him; and so, by the same notion being entertained by all separately, the common cause imperceptibly decays.[106]

This overuse of common resources is reminiscent of the myth of Erysichthon where the Mediterranean's great forests are cut down by Greece and Troy to build the boats and engines of war. In his book on politics, Aristotle (ca. 322 B.C.) also commented on the problem, explaining:

> All persons call the same thing mine and the sense in which each does so may be a fine thing, but it is impracticable; or if the words are taken in the other sense, such a unity in no way conduces to harmony. And there is an-

---

[104] Forster Lloyd, Two Lectures on the Checks to Population.
[105] Garrett Hardin, "The Tragedy of the Commons," In *Science,* vol. 62, no. 3859 (Dec. 13, 1968), pp. 1243ff.
[106] History of the Peloponnesian War, Book 1, sec. 141.

other objection to the proposal. For that which is common to the greatest number has the least care bestowed upon it. Every one thinks chiefly of his own, hardly at all of the common interest; and only when he is himself concerned as an individual. For besides other considerations, everybody is more inclined to neglect the duty which he expects another to fulfill.[107]

These words are equally applicable today. One of our greatest problems is acknowledging that the earth is now "the common interest." With so many self-interests, how can humanity think collectively in a way that does not destroy the common environment? Initially, industrialized society was developed in the common interest of making human life easier, yet the introduction of machines during the Industrial Revolution produced wastes on a much larger scale than the earth could process.

The Industrial Revolution

The Industrial Revolution brought about profound changes that began in British society, then rapidly spread throughout Europe and later to the United States.[108] In the late eighteenth and early nineteenth centuries, machines replaced the manual-labor based economy. All of daily life changed in some way, and the mechanization that started in the textile industry led to developments in iron-working techniques and created a demand for coal. This in turn forced the development of transportation via steam power and steam-powered machines. Further developments in this area led to steamships and eventually to internal combustion engines and electrical power generators.

The explosive growth of industry in England and the U.S. led to an associated growth in industrial wastes. It is not unreasonable to assume that the generation of waste produced between 1850 and 2008 in Europe and the U.S. will be reproduced in developing countries, particularly India and China, in the coming years.

A series of *New York Times* articles since 2008 describe India and China's industrialized pollution, increased need for food, and desire for

---

[107] See *Politics,* Book II, chap. III, 1261b
[108] See Pat Hudson, The Industrial Revolution, and Stewart Ross, The Industrial Revolution.

the "goods" of the West.[109] The Asian economy's growing demand for energy will increase the externalization of local wastes, thus stressing or destroying soil and water recourses. It will also increase greenhouse gas emissions such as carbon dioxide, oxides of nitrogen and sulphur. China has stated that it will bring one coal-fired power plant on line each week for the next two years. The plants do not have the pollution-control devices found in the U.S. or Europe, and there are no international laws in place requiring them. The amount of energy needed to sustain the world's population today versus the population of 1850, especially with all the necessary accoutrements of modern life, is daunting. Without pollution control devices in place, one can see how the outcome of such development could be devastating.

In *The Making of an English Landscape,* W. G. Hoskins describes the changing English landscape before and after Enclosure in the 1850s. The reorganization and redistribution of small tracts of land into larger parcels made the land more productive, but took management out of the hands of individual farmers who used the Commons. The so-called poor quality Commons then became a place to dump wastes. The smoke stacks had no controls and the buildings of towns such as Sheffield, Wigan and Newcastle became black because of the use of coal. The land around towns with glass works, chemical works and coalmines became sterile moonscapes—dead and lifeless. Hoskins's descriptions of the early destructive acts of the era are a good model for other times and locations because they took place in an island country and culture.

Once the population reaches a critical mass on an island, there is little room for expansion and one person's externalized waste very quickly becomes another's personal waste problem. This is reminiscent of the symbol of the cell discussed earlier and the biological system that became overloaded with waste. An island is like a small chemical reactor where things can heat up quickly. Interactions between reactants in the vessel are immediate and problems become apparent more readily. Islands are good predictors of issues that can occur on continents and ultimately worldwide because the Earth is an island in space. At the moment, restrictions on garbage collection in Britain have led to new con-

---

109 See *NewYork Times* (online), 2008a.

flicts, which the government hopes will challenge their society to reconsider what they use and how they dispose of wastes. At one point there were stories of people receiving high fines for overloading their garbage cans or sneaking their excess garbage into their neighbors' cans. In some places, individuals were reported storing their garbage because there aren't places to dispose of it. Here is an example of a modern-day island attempting to find a solution to the fact that it can no longer contain the waste its population produces.

In an expansive country like the United States, historically the population has generally had the option to move West to escape the overcrowding and industrialization on the East Coast. This became known as our Manifest Destiny—the idea that we have a right to move West because "God told us to." As the population in the U.S. increases and available land is consumed and overbuilt, the conflicts between industry and the individual will increase. Due to the amount of space that was previously available in the U.S., few environmental controls were needed. There seemed to be sufficient land to extract resources and leave waste behind without impacting society. As industrialization has increased, however, the wastes of the past now affect the residents of the present, and the need for environmental controls has become apparent. To protect the individual from historical waste dumps and hazardous chemicals, the first major environmental law in the U.S. was passed—the Comprehensive Environmental Response Compensation and Liability Act (CERCLA, also called Superfund) was designed to force any person or entity associated with dumping waste to pay for its cleanup and any human or environmental damage it may have caused. I say more about this later.

The Psychology of Externalization

All animals externalize metabolic waste products from their body. The human mother deals with the wastes until her children are developmentally ready to deal with the wastes themselves. According to Freud, at the age of one to one and one-half years a child enters the anal stage. During toilet training, a child is aware of the erogenous zone of the anus and with the retention or expulsion of the feces. This represents a classic conflict between the id, which derives pleasure from the expulsion of bodily wastes, and the ego and superego, which derive pleasure from adhering to practical and societal pressures in order to control bodily functions.

During the anal stage, a child's desires are in conflict with the parents' demands. The child can fight the parent and refuse to go to the bathroom, or mind the parent. The child who wants to fight takes pleasure in excreting maliciously, perhaps just before being placed on the toilet. If the child derives pleasure and success from this expulsion, it is thought to result in the formation of an anal expulsive character. This character is generally messy, disorganized, reckless, careless, and defiant. Conversely, a child who opts to retain feces, thereby spiting his parents while enjoying the pleasurable pressure of the built-up feces within his colon, may develop an anal retentive character. This character is neat, precise, orderly, careful, stingy, withholding, obstinate, meticulous, and passive-aggressive. Freudian theory suggests that the resolution of the anal stage, which includes proper toilet training, permanently affects the individual's propensities toward possession and attitudes toward authority. This stage lasts from one and one-half to two years.

The externalization of waste and pollution on the land can also be viewed through a developmental psychology lens. During the Industrial Revolution there were no authority figures to prevent the externalization (dumping) of wastes into the environment. Reforms came into being only after pollution, disease and quality of life became unbearable. The London "pea-soup fogs" in the early to mid-1900s, and the dead River Thames, became indicators of England's poor environmental quality. If we examine the dates of these occurrences, the Industrial Revolution is clearly the root cause of these events, and the laws designed to clean up the pollution were only enacted after a long waiting period. Owners of industry were the most resistant, much like a child's resistance to toilet training. This resistance continues today as industrialized nations move their manufacturing to countries like China that have lower standards or no environmental restrictions. This lack of responsibility to nature shows how greed and resistance can supersede all.

The same pattern occurred in the United States from 1850 to the 1960s. During this time, wastes were dumped into landfills, waste pits, rivers and oceans. It was not until the 1962 publication of *Silent Spring* by Rachel Carson that environmental issues came to public attention. Carson's book chronicles the effects of pesticides on wildlife and her description of rapid species loss was astonishing. It brought about a change in the way the U.S. dealt with dumping. Carson is an example of how one individual's efforts can make huge changes in the perception of the collective. Her campaign against DDT resulted in a ban of the substance in developing countries, where it was probably the safest and most effective pesticide for controlling insect-borne diseases like malaria.[110]

Following Carson's book, people began to speak up and the so-called developed world started to pay more attention to its impact on nature. More environmental regulations came into being. For example, power station emissions from coal-fired plants in the American northeast were designed to prevent damage in Canada. Meanwhile, restrictions on releases from the industrial Rhine valley were designed to prevent deforestation of the Black Forest caused by acid rain.

As the Asian block (China and India) develops their industrial capabilities, the externalization of wastes will increase. If developmental psychology is a guide, pressure from the West to decrease externalization will be met with resistance. Metaphorically, the West is trying to learn from its mistakes and potty-train the developing countries. Those countries that perceive a threat to their financial well-being or sense of self-determination will resist. Also, like the skeptics in the West, many people in developing industrial countries may not value or understand the need to decrease the externalization of wastes in order to curtail global climate change. While their actions and goals seem to be based more on the drive to survive rather than greed, developing countries appear disconnected from nature and ignorant of how interconnected the earth is as an interdependent system, or ecosystem.

The Psychology of Environmental Problems

The externalization of wastes by industrial and developing nations into the earth, seas and air is common practice. We ignore the potential impacts of these releases. As individuals we may have conflicted feelings about these effects that we choose to ignore because to act would

---

[110] See Lovelock, *The Revenge of Gaia,* p. 108.

threaten our financial well-being or societal status. As a community of individuals we may also choose to ignore these effects because they might disrupt our social fabric. A psychological origin for our inability or reluctance to confront environmental issues can be seen in many of the approaches recognized by contemporary psychologists.[111]

According to James Hillman, "There is only one core issue in psychology. *"Where is the 'me'?* Where does the 'me' begin? Where does the 'me' stop"? Where does the *'other'* begin?"[112] For the individual, Hillman is correct in that we explore the interiority of ourselves in relation to the other, and the psychology of environmental problems challenges us, where we can, to look at our effects on nature as "other." The ego psychologist's approach to individual psychology is briefly summarized below. However, for a corporate industrial entity the goal is to survive and expand, make a profit and pay dividends. There is no "psychological interiority." The "me-ness" of the entity is dependent on the psyches of individuals around the Boardroom table and the environmental charter is mandated from the interiority of these particular individuals. It is here where the individual has the greatest impact. This factor is relevant where I discuss the Cultural Complex later in this book.

When we are presented with environmental problems, Freudian psychology would suggest that defenses of the ego could be relevant. That is, when the ego is confronted with information that it finds too uncomfortable, it will employ defenses to avoid the psychological discomfort. Higher-level defenses include intellectualization and rationalization. Activities such as cost-benefit analysis and comparative risk assessment are techniques used when setting environmental regulations that employ these types of defenses. Lower level defenses such as idealization, projection and fantasy might be employed to distort the magnitude of environmental problems, or to project them onto others. For major issues, such as global warming, species loss and the actual magnitude of BP/Transoceanic's oil spill in the Gulf, pathological levels of defense are often employed. These include denial, distortion, splitting, and the delu-

---

111 See Deborah Du Nann Winter and Susan Koger, "The Psychology of Environmental Problems."
112 Hillman, "A Psyche the Size of the Earth," in T. Roszak, ed., *Ecopsychology,* p. xvii.

sional projection of the causes of our own problems onto others.

Federal, state and local governments have employed behavioral psychology for many years to modify human behavior in favor of nature. Public littering laws have discouraged poor behavior with fines and social pressure, encouraged good behavior with receptacles and recycling programs. Air quality and pollution prevention laws have required a reduction in air pollution releases, and yet air levels of greenhouse gases increase. The world's nations toy with carbon credits and emissions quotas and yet no agreements are reached.

Cognitive psychology, which can be broadly defined as the psychology of mental processes, attempts to find intelligent or thought-based solutions to environmental problems. For example, sustainability is an attempt to find solutions that respond to the needs of nature while including the needs of community or society in which the pollution occurs, and the industry that is responsible for polluting and paying for cleanup. Human health and ecological risk assessment fit within the area of cognitive psychology because it is an attempt to find a compromise solution that protects as many interests as possible. One problem with a cognitive psychological approach to many of the world's pollution problems is that they no longer impact locally. For example, China's air quality problems impact Los Angeles, American industrial smoke stacks impacted Canada, and a National Center for Atmospheric Research model of the BP/Transoceanic oil spill in the Gulf of Mexico has been predicted to impact every U.S. seaboard state and Canada.

Ecopsychology is a psychology, or philosophy, which believes humanity is connected to nature through a primal part of the psyche called the "ecological unconscious." From a Jungian perspective, this ecological unconscious is similar to the Nature archetype. However, according to Jung, nature is the unconscious, yet the idea is consistent with Jung's original concepts. However, ecopsychology is an animistic psychology; it believes we have an inner animal part, and attempts to connect individuals to this, believing that a reconnection to nature can heal our wounded psyche. In contrast to ego-centered psychologies, ecopsychology does not believe this can be done through a cognitive process; it is rather a process that requires a feeling connection to nature.

In contrast to ego-oriented approaches to environmental problems and their potential solutions, Jung's analytical psychology views the problems from the perspective of the ego, but through an archetypal lens. Jung's complex theory, discussed earlier, indicates that we are likely to form complexes around environmental issues because they cause internal psychic conflict. That is, we are torn between the conscious part of the ego-complex that is required to function—to live, eat, travel, reproduce and eliminate waste—and the unconscious, which is linked to our instinctive awareness that we are damaging the earth. The ego dislikes this conflict and relegates the issues to the shadow; that is, forms a complex that remains unconscious until it is constellated.

On an archetypal level, we are linked through our personal unconscious to the collective unconscious and our mythic roots. On some level we understand that we are damaging nature and fail to act. However, many individuals actively campaign against environmentalism in all of its forms. In the scientific community, this often means relying on science to refute, or argue against, the prevailing weight of evidence. Typically this means picking apart scientific papers on a point-by-point basis, or siding with uncertainty to undermine a finding. "Collect more data," is the rallying cry and the issues go unresolved. This is confounding unless one considers that an archetypal defense system may be operating.

In 1996, Donald Kalsched published *The Inner World of Trauma,* a book in which he describes, from a Jungian perspective, how early childhood trauma can cause the formation of a persecutor-protector complex, which he names "the self-care system." When an individual is confronted with such trauma, the psyche splits and a more sensitive part of the psyche withdraws behind a type of shell for protection by the self-care system. The other part of the psyche protects this inner part by becoming hardened to the attacks and insults that caused or aggravated the original split. From Kalsched's perspective, this system is vigilant against all attacks, and at some point prevents the wounded inner core of the psyche from reaching out for connection to the world.

Just as the system worked so elegantly to keep the individual safe in childhood, it also isolates and becomes persecutory toward this inner part. This paradoxical double bind continues into adulthood unless the individual begins to investigate the system.

Given our reluctance to act on behalf of nature, one has to wonder if, on an archetypal level in the psyche, this predetermined psychological trauma response channel is not activated in response to environmental trauma. Paradoxically, our loss of connection with nature through Enclosure, the Industrial Revolution, urbanization and a nihilist postmodern life, and our constant lack of connection to a sense of place through relocation, has caused what I would call a nature-trauma. The inner part of us that reveres and cherishes nature is split off behind a self-care system where the protector part now functions to keep us isolated and safe from a true understanding of the effects we have on nature. When we try to connect to natural disasters, the self-care system becomes persecutory and attacks us, keeping our attitude in line with the collective, with industry and with our current way of life. Change is impossible without creative interventions. Environmental disasters like the BP/Transoceanic, Exxon Valdiz and Amoco Cadiz oil spills only serve to reinforce our protector part and keep us from connecting in a deeply meaningful way to the unfolding traumas. This archetypal defense system is a powerful inner force telling us oil is a necessary evil, that we can recover from spills, that nothing is really being harmed, and the species loss is also not significant. The protective defense expands to "who needs polar bears," or "there are no problems with nuclear waste."

The archetypal self-care system is a tenacious mechanism that convinces us to look no further because our separation from and objectification of nature is the very definition of "progress." This attitude interrupts and impairs our ability to imagine alternatives. We become one-sided, and foreclose on possible solutions or opportunities that would benefit both humanity and the earth.

In the case studies to be introduced later, group dynamics are discussed and I propose that this archetypal defense mechanism may be active in groups in conflict over environmental issues. Kalsched's work has been suggested to apply to the Kouretes (a group) protecting baby Zeus.

The same dynamics so elegantly described by Kalsched (1996) may come alive in the traumatized group psyche as well as in the private horror of a traumatized individual. The traumatized group may develop a cohort of

74

protector/persecutor leaders who function like the *Kouretes* protecting Baby Zeus or the Cuban American relatives protecting Elian Gonzales. The traumatized group spirit may well be subject to the same nurturing protection and/or violent torture and at the hands of its *Daimones* leaders. All of the group's defenses mobilized in the name of the self care system which is designed to protect the injured divine child of the group identity, as well as to protect the group "ego" from a terrifying sense of imminent annihilation.[113]

From the perspective of the Nature archetype, humanity has been made more aware of how our actions in the industrialized world have impacted the planet and our future. The Nature archetype is instilling consciousness. It may be exerting an effect on us through the changes that are being observed by scientists and environmental engineers. The experience of hazardous waste, environmental destruction or species loss may constellate a sense of alienation and pending annihilation in the psyche that is an expression of this archetype.

Nature Deprivation

Our attachment to nature is deeply rooted, like the tree that holds itself firmly in the deep dark earth. Humanity is part of nature; we live in the natural world and depend on it fully, every day. Trees and plants surround us. We eat animal and vegetable life that is fed by the sun. We are dependent on nature for our existence and without it we would not survive. Sadly, many inner city children have never touched a goat, milked a cow or placed their hands under the warm body and bony feet of a chicken to retrieve a fresh warm egg.

This lack of early contact with the numinous quality of these experiences leads to nature-deprived children. Not unlike Pentheus, we consider ourselves somehow separate from or above nature. Yet we still need nature to provide for us. Archetypal patterns emerge more clearly when humanity is confronted by events that are archetypal, such as the effects of waste and climate change that threaten our survival.

In the following chapter I discuss some hazardous waste impacts.

---

113 Thomas Singer and Samuel Kimbles, *The Cultural Complex,* p. 19.

5

Case Studies

Tragedy demands that choices be made among alternatives; comedy assumes that all choice is likely to be in error and that survival depends upon finding accommodation that will permit all parties to endure.[114]

As postindustrial humanity studies the Earth, it is profoundly obvious that something is wrong. Species are dying at an alarming rate, the average temperature of the globe is increasing, and global weather patterns have changed. These changes correlate with increased industrial activity, carbon dioxide levels and other key indicators that point to an increase in greenhouse gases.[115] On a microscale, in "your own back-yard," there has been an increase in the levels of chemicals released into the environment each year for the past century. Many of these chemicals do not easily degrade in the environment and thus accumulate in biological species, a process called bioaccumulation.[116] Often the same chemicals that bioaccumulate act as hormonal (endocrine) disruptors.[117] They look and act like the body's chemical messenger system (hormones), which interfere with biological messages in the body and so cause cancer or other hormone-regulated problems now being investigated by the Environmental Protection Agency (EPA).[118] We have known about the dangers of these chemicals since Carson's *Silent Spring* was published in 1962.

It may be that the human psychological defenses identified by Freud (denial, repression and projection) are operating to prevent us from seeing some of the basic facts and interfere with us making adjustments and changes. Or is it, as Eliade suggests, that control of these resources is in the hands of a few who resist change? Since both these paradigms offer

---

114 J. W. Meeker, *The Comedy of Survival,* p. 33.
115 See J. Houghton, *Global Warming,* and S. Schneider, *Global Warming.*
116 See B. Beek, Bioaccumulation: New Aspects and Developments, p. 4.
117 See M. Metzler, *Endocrine Disruptors,* part I, p. 3.
118 "Review of the EPA's Proposed Environmental Endocrine Disruptor Screening Program," EPA-SAB-EC-99-013.

something useful, it is probably "both/and," emphasized by the lack of pragmatic knowledge or imagination about what to do next.

On a collective level, there are ideas for change, although they often feel polarized into opposites. On one side there are those who suggest that we should return to a mythic view of the world, where we see the Earth as Gaia, a whole organism to be revered and protected. If it cannot be returned to its pristine purity, it must be kept safe. On the other hand, there are those who argue that our environmental contamination is being blown out of proportion and that nature is resilient. A recent fictional book, *State of Fear*, by Michael Crichton has popularized the idea that the scientists have it wrong and that the problem with global climate change is actually a statistical problem. There are others who believe that whatever problems we may have are resolvable with technology: humans can, and should, control nature.

However, when we see environmental problems framed in a polarization into two sides, creating a tension of the opposites, it is the mark of a complex. The complex has an archetypal core and indicates the presence of the Nature archetype.

Jung's model of individuation adds insight to our understanding of the Nature archetype.[119] In "The Psychology of the Child Archetype," Jung addresses the futurity of the archetype and sees the motif of the child as signifying the anticipation of future developments: "In the individuation process, it anticipates the figure that comes from the synthesis of conscious and unconscious elements in the personality. It is therefore a symbol which unites the opposites." The child is not the only symbol that unites the opposites, and Jung has described the importance of uniting the opposites,[120] and the process by which the opposites can be united into another form of wholeness. "I have called this wholeness that transcends conscious the "self.""[121]

By holding the tension of the opposites, a third, a transcendent view, is

---

119 "The Psychology of the Child Archetype," *The Archetypes and the Collective Unconscious*, CW 9i, par. 278.
120 See "The Significance of the Uniting Symbol," *Psychological Types*, CW 6, pars. 318ff.
121 "The Psychology of the Child Archetype," *The Archetypes of the Collective Unconscious*, CW 9i, par. 278.

produced by the Self to resolve the tension by expanding the ego. For the collective, holding a tension between the past (represented by abundant oil) and the future (represented by no oil or modern conveniences), it is difficult to see how a transcendent position may come about. But it is my assertion that the Self, acting through the Nature archetype and its influence on the imagination of the individual, can introduce transcendent solutions that are often a combination of the technological and the mythic. The individual can then influence collective groups that hold similar intentions or views. This vessel of imagination leads to the creation of resolutions that expand collective consciousness and solve environmental problems.

The process of being forced to hold a tension of opposing forces both between groups, and in the individual psyche, when attempting to resolve environmental problems and preserve nature, is consistent with the dynamic that operates with the "cultural complex," as described by Kimbles:

> Cultural complex dynamics operate at the group level of the psyche of the individual and within the dynamics of group life. They are expressions of deeply help beliefs and emotions that are characteristically expressed through both group and individual representations, images, affects, patterns and practices. Cultural complexes play out in the intermediate area between the archetypal layer of the psyche on the one hand and the more personal level of unconscious life on the other. Through the activity of these complexes belonging to a larger cultural whole, the individual has a feeling of belonging to a specific group with a specific identity.[122]

The modern-day case histories that I examine in this chapter have mythic themes and potential solutions to the tension of the opposites caused by environmental problems.

Cases Background

I was intimately involved with site investigations, determination of cleanup goals, and advising on the cleanup process for the environmental damage in the following case studies. I was also responsible for, or involved with, risk communication meetings and town hall meetings where

---

[122] Samuel Kimbles, *The Cultural Complex*, p. 199.

discussions took place and resolutions emerged. In many ways, I played a role of analyst when working in these environments, assessing and treating the problems through a thorough in-depth investigation.

These case studies further illustrate the theme of nature and the resolution of conflict (tension of opposites) in service to the Nature archetype. The central tool used in each case is a risk assessment process. These cases are common and important not so much to show that science can play a role in cleaning up the environment, but because they demonstrate that individuals have a special connection with nature. It is our love of nature that wells up from inside, from the Self, and this upwelling drives and/or encourages us all to act in ways that benefit others or nature. Having been to hundreds of public meetings, I know that it is ultimately the voice of individuals who have the courage to speak out, even when they think they will not be heard or their position will not fit in with the collective, that initiates the individuation journey.

These stories also reflect an environmental imagination, flawed in the sense that what the imagination proposes cannot immediately restore the environment to its previous pristine condition. Yet the individual's imagination and courage to consider possibilities are examples of the Self in action that constellates adjustments in the psyche. The case studies illustrate the attempts to liberate nature from the shroud of industrial waste. In society today, the Nature archetype represents both the nurturing side of the feminine and the steward (the shepherd, forester or farmer) side of the masculine. These stories are about an individual's relationship with the unconscious and with the Self, with each other, and with nature.

Superfund

One of the first hazardous waste sites that I investigated in the U.S., early in my environmental career, was the former Manufactured Gas Plant in Lowell, Massachusetts. This plant was built to fuel the textile mills of the Northeast. It manufactured town gas (carbon monoxide) from coal, then oil. The wastes were dumped into the Lowell canal in addition to waste pits on- and off-site, and were then sold to entrepreneurs who used the wastes as foundation support under Lowell residences. The dumping started in the 1850s and wastes were still present in the 1990s. These wastes are the same as those seen in England's Industrial Revolution and include coal tar, petroleum wastes, cyanide and metals. The process by which these wastes were addressed became the Comprehensive Environmental Response, Compensation, and Liability Act (CERCLA) and the associated National Contingency Plan of the 1980s.

Lawsuits against Lowell Power and Light (now Colonial Gas) for cyanide contamination underneath these Lowell homes funded Jan Schlickman's lawsuit against Grace Chemical, depicted in the film *A Civil Action,* based on the book by Jonathan Harr. CERCLA holds that any company or individual who has owned, generated, transported or disposed of a waste illegally is liable even if they are not responsible for the dumping (joint and several liability). The law is far reaching and curtails illegal dumping because of the cost of punitive awards and civil lawsuits. CERCLA attorneys such as Schlickman have been successful in enforcing this law. However, the law only relates to illegal dumping, and release of many millions of tons of wastes is still permitted.

Superfund was so named because of the large sums of money that is set aside to pay for cleanup contamination when the original perpetrators or owners cannot be found. When the environmental law was developed by the Ronald Regan presidency, it came under attack. Rita Lavelle, an industry-biased Environmental Protection Agency (EPA) administrator, prevented full implementation of the law. This caused a backlash. Former EPA administrator William Ruckelshaus was then appointed to the post and replaced Lavelle. He was able to implement Superfund, with its "joint and several" liability provision, meaning that any person or entity with so-called deep pockets pays for the cleanup regardless of how much waste they may have contributed, or how guilty they might be. If any individual or company has a hand in generating, handling, transporting or disposing of any part of the waste associated with a site, that individual or company can be held responsible for the cost of cleaning up *all* of the waste.

Superfund was considered punitive and expensive by industry, but for the most part it was effective in addressing the worst hazardous waste sites in the U.S. For the first time, improper disposal of industrial waste became, and still is, against the law. Unfortunately, successive Bush administrations and Republican Congresses have taken the teeth out of Superfund by failing to refill its depleted coffers and reducing enforcement. This dilution of Superfund has brought the country back to the years prior to the 1980s. The fear of environmental litigation has reduced the most flagrant contraventions, but it is nature that still bears the brunt of the environmental impacts.

Central to all environmental laws (including Superfund) is a process called risk assessment, which seeks to determine if a substance has a risk or hazard that should be mitigated before it harms human health or the environment. Rather than cleaning up everything everywhere, a logos-oriented "cost benefit" analysis process is undertaken to determine what most needs to be cleaned and to what level. All such analyses are subjective. The pragmatism of postmodern industrial life balances the cost to industry versus the amount of dumping that is considered acceptable. Cleanup is now based on a balance between cost and risk, with human health and environmental risk assessment as the fulcrum about which it turns. The process is designed to protect over ninety-five percent of the population. The health of the remaining five percent is essentially sacrificed to the economics of dealing with large populations.

The process of investigating a site or environmental problem is broken into steps for ease of investigation, budgeting, communication and cleanup. The risk assessment process is central to Superfund and has four steps:

1. To investigate and identify chemicals that present a risk.

2. To identify who might be exposed to the chemicals and how.

3. To identify the toxic effects of the chemicals in human and environmental receptors.

4. To quantify the risks to human health, the environment and the associated uncertainty.[123]

Ruckelshaus reported that it was not adequate for government to simply calculate the risk for hazardous wastes, but that the results of the risk

---

[123] See Ecological Risk Assessment Guidance for Superfund: Process for Designing and Conducting Ecological Risk Assessments, EPA 540—R-97-006, and Risk Assessment Guidance for Superfund, vol. I, Human Health Evaluation Manual, EPA 540—1-89/002.

calculation process must be clearly communicated to the public, especially the affected communities. In addition to the technical elements of risk assessment, Ruckelshaus wanted the process to involve public meetings and community outreach programs, which would explain the findings and develop a remedial action plan.

He called this new process risk communication. It requires the active involvement of affected communities in the cleaning up of hazardous wastes in their midst. Risk communication brings relationship, eros, to a previously logos-oriented and power-dominated process. Regulations used to be enacted and cleanups carried out without input or agreement from the affected parties. The directive to communicate requires that the scientists and engineers who are involved with mapping the problem and defining the solutions must involve the affected communities, and to some degree seek agreement from them. Superfund did not go so far as to give decision-making authority to the public, but it did help to alleviate the sense of helplessness in the communities where the waste was found. Thus, risk communication became a field of study and aspects of the work have been incorporated into the field of ecopsychology.[124]

The process of investigation reduces anxiety associated with the site. Using Freud's structure of the psyche (id, ego and superego), the id would represent the unknown or unconscious aspects of the situation. That is, we are unconscious of the exact extent of our risk and our defenses stimulate our ego into believing it has no control and we are powerless and unsafe. The ego does not know the reality of the situation and it is anxious about its safety. The superego is looking for control over this unstable process. Or, consistent with Jung's theories, the presence of hazardous substances stimulates a complex in the unconscious and we may become overwhelmed by the complex. It is only when the ego is supplied with enough concrete information to assess the danger that the power of the complex dissipates.

Risk communication is the process through which the ego is satisfied and the complex deactivated. There are parallels with the risk communication process and Jungian analysis. To some extent, the process in-

---

[124] See National Research Council, *Improving Risk Communication,* and J. Macy, "Working Through Environmental Despair," in T. Roszak, ed., *Ecopsychology.*

volves working with the shadow, where we are required to face and understand the severity of the feared unknown, so that we can remedy the problem by living with the potential impacts to our health, our psyche, or both. Jung said: "It is everybody's allotted fate to become conscious of and learn to deal with this shadow."[125] By working with the shadow we uncover innovative solutions to problems. The process also requires that we resolve our relationship with nature. We must confront our personal values and be clear how nature fits into our lives. This process, although not completely satisfactory, activates the Nature archetype that responds with the psychic energy that fuels us in dealing with these issues.

The communication efforts involved with alerting residents that their homes were built on cyanide wastes were challenging, especially when the form of cyanide in the soil was a conspicuous bright blue (ferrocyanide-complex). Psychologically, the residents' complexes were fear-based, primal and overwhelming. The constellated complex was heightened when the resident had children or pets. Although the residents received compensation and the homes were remediated, many used the money to leave the property.

BP/Amoco, Casper, Wyoming

The former BP/Amoco refinery is a four-hundred-acre petroleum-refining facility built in 1913. It is located on the banks of the North Platte River on the southwest side of Casper, Wyoming. The refinery operated for more than eighty years and played a major role in both the city and state economies. During operations, liquid was disposed of in the river and sludge was pumped into an artificial lake called Soda Lake. When operations ended in 1991, the site was contaminated with nearly eighty years worth of oil spillage, sludge and more than two hundred miles of buried pipeline. The property was fenced and abandoned.

In 1996 and 1997, a group of local citizens sued for impacts to their properties. The state of Wyoming intervened in this lawsuit. As part of the settlement agreement, the state of Wyoming and BP/Amoco signed a consent decree that became the basis for cleanup at the site. The property is now divided into three different areas: the south properties (revitalized

---

125 "The Fight with the Shadow," *Civiliazation in Transition,* CW 10, par. 455.

into the Platte River Commons), the north properties (Salt Creek Heights Business Center), and Soda Lake (a major migratory bird habitat and resting area along the Central Migratory Bird Flyway). This particular cleanup is interesting because of two pivotal, innovative agreements. First, the company and the state of Wyoming established a collaborative process to aid the cleanup. Second, a Re-use Agreement between BP-Amoco and the City of Casper and Natrona County created a re-use partnership linked to reasonable, protective and timely cleanup. The city and county appointed a group of citizens, a Joint Powers Board, to manage the Re-use Agreement.

Early in the process the EPA was involved and divisions between BP/Amoco and EPA landed the parties in Federal Court where the Judge ordered the parties to reach agreement or the Court would mandate a path forward. The collaborative agreement was acceptable to the Court, but applied adequate pressure, heating the negotiated investigation process.

In 2002, Casper chose a cleanup procedure that linked cleanup and re-use with an ambitious three-year deadline to reach a reasonable final remedy for the entire site.[126] Innovative technologies were used to communicate complex technical data to the public and to clean up the four hundred acres including oil-cleaning wetlands and bioremediation.[127] The cleanup plans included a golf course, a river kayak course, a civic center for the River Commons, a business park, and a migratory bird habitat for the former sludge lagoon at Soda Lake.

From a psychological perspective, the city of Casper was party to the contamination in their midst. Some of the people who attended the meetings were former employees and managers who had worked at the refinery. They confessed their part in the dumping of liquid tar into the river and the release onto the soil of liquid lead-metal solutions from a vast underground pool called the "swimming pool." Others talked of their many hours watching osprey hunt and nest above the river during the time when the river was polluted and the sorrow they felt in their hearts for these birds. Their connection to the land and to nature was obvious. There were long public meetings and volumes of reports documenting

---

[126] See *Casper, 2005* (online).
[127] See *Wetlands, 2006* (online).

the results of investigations and cleanup strategies. Linking the cleanup to environmental restoration deadlines ensured that the hazards did not remain longer than necessary, but it also required human effort to keep on top of it.

Members of the Audubon Society and other non-governmental organizations pushed for a re-inclusion of nature back into the process. One man envisioned reforming an open body of water for the migratory birds that he had seen when he was a child. It seemed that a deep passion dwelled within the heart of this man and within the hearts of many people who were willing and dedicated to join him in the collaborative process. I believe the Nature archetype was moving through them, and their feeling for nature influenced their actions. Nature was restored to some degree—the bird corridor was protected and restored, the river was re-shaped and ospreys have returned.

Yet, the results of this type of cleanup process are not perfect. A golf course is not pristine land, nor does it reflect a natural landscape, but the land has moved from black and brown to green. In addition, the migrating birds will not pick up tar and die on their journey across the country. The key issue in this project included the collaborative process where everyone was invited to participate and where all voices could be heard.

We can view this cleanup process as the shadow becoming conscious, and after due consideration it can be integrated into the psyche. Similar to Jungian analysis, the psyche experiences an increase in healthy creative energy when the shadow is made conscious and integrated. It provided an opportunity for some "truth and reconciliation" with nature. The community was given a seat at the table and from that seat they expressed their concerns and their imagination for the future. The process allowed the community to come together, form new working relationships, and become familiar with various viewpoints, experiences and possibilities.

This collaborative problem-solving process is now central to the Wyoming Voluntary Cleanup Program.[128]

---

128 See *Wyoming, 2008* (online).

Mining in Butte, Montana started in the 1870s. The town flourished with the discovery of silver and copper. Copper deposits are so rich here that mining continues today. The town of Anaconda processed the ore into copper and as a result, mine tailings and smelter wastes were dumped into the Silver Bow Creek that flowed into the Clark Fork River. Over time, these wastes mixed with soil and natural sediments to form the riverbed of the Clark Fork River. Montana Power built a cofferdam and hydroelectric power station at the confluence of the Clark Fork and Blackfoot Rivers a few miles upstream of Missoula, in western Montana. The contaminated sediments collected behind the dam to form the Milltown Reservoir Sediments Superfund Site (Milltown Site), which is part of the larger Clark Fork River Superfund Site. Approximately 6.6 million cubic yards of contaminated sediments collected behind the dam, polluting the local drinking water aquifer with releases of arsenic and copper that also threatened fish and other aquatic life.[129]

Following extensive investigations that included studies of human health issues in the reservoir, the river, the groundwater, and people's homes, it was determined that the sediments should be cleaned up and the dam removed. There was broad public support for this cleanup plan. Ninety-eight percent of the nearly 5,000 comments received on the cleanup plan during the public comment period supported the EPA's proposed solution. The investigation of the Atlantic Richfield Company (ARCO) dam started in 1990 and lasted about three years. Combining the data collected during this period with the data from an earlier study conducted in the 1980s, it was recommended that selected sediments and the dam be removed. The dam was finally breached on March 23, 2008, allowing the river to flow freely once again.[130].

Through the process of managing the investigation, I came to know many of the residents of Milltown and Bonner Junction, a small settlement next to the reservoir. The risk-assessment process required that we take dust samples from inside their homes, soil from their vegetable gar-

---

[129] See EPA, 2008, *The Milltown Superfund Site,* update (online).
[130] *New York Times,* 2008b (online).

dens and even the vegetables themselves to analyze them for lead, arsenic and other toxic metals. Residents experienced this sampling as invasive, and it made them realize that there was a potential risk to their lives and the lives of their children. It brought home that they could be at risk for cancer or other health problems. My young sampling crew and I often became the focal point for the residents' anger at this invasion of chemicals and our subsequent research of it. We carried the shadow and our team became the scapegoat for what had gone wrong in the community for many years. The lack of safety in their own homes logically led to the distrust of and anger at anyone who invaded their property or happened to be the bearer of bad news.

One of the problems of communicating with victims of exposure to waste is that "those most strongly motivated to communicate about risk are often those with the strongest interest in the decisions."[131] That is, those paid to communicate are often consultants and government officials—who are seen as biased and just wanting the problem to be gone—or the industry that created the problem. Investigating organizations, responsible parties and consultants are seen as "hired guns" who are paid to lie for the polluter. So distrust of the communication process is always high. This dynamic is consistent with the double bind of the personal psychological self-care system, where the regulators, who should be seen as the protectors of the environment, are seen as the persecutors.

Local residents and those further downstream from Missoula were happy when the river again ran freely after the dam was removed. This was an attempt to restore the area "as closely as possible" to its original condition. Many people resolved that the original condition could not be achieved in the short term. It had taken over a hundred and thirty years for the problem to come about. Due to the type of contamination, it was obvious that a quick fix was not possible. However, there was an intention to fix the problem and a growing imagination and belief within the collective that change could and would occur. Ultimately, there was a restoration of the environment that people could live with. The movie *A River Runs Through It*, set on the Blackfoot River a few miles above Milltown, represents this original condition and beauty of the land. When

---

131 National Research Council, *Improving Risk Communication*, p. 115.

I spoke with local residents, they all hoped for such beauty to be returned to Milltown. The imaginative film presented an idealized image for the collective to hold on to.

The responsible party for the investigation and cleanup had a distinct incentive to resist significant change because of the cost. They were also responsible for the original source of the contamination, the Berkeley pit, Warms Spring Ponds and the 125 miles of Clark Fork River system. The mining industry still had close ties with State government and significant political power. Local small town residents felt the power differential. In addition to the constelled feelings of fear and powerlessness, if they worked for the mining company, there were also conflicting feelings of guilt and shame as part of the environmental complex.

A River Runs Through It represents an expression of the deeper Nature archetype that brings people together with a commitment to restore and clean up nature and the environment. Even though they knew that the pristine scenes shown in the film were unattainable, it gave the community a collective screen for their projections and united them in a powerful way. Imagining what it *could* be like brought these people into communication around a central theme rooted in a respect for nature and the creative energy associated with renewal. They wanted nature restored, so removing the dam became a symbol of that restoration. The process offered them a sense of agency through remembering and supporting nature, and healing some of the feelings of powerlessness that had preceded the cleanup process. Powerful mining interests had previously dumped wastes into the community, but now the community no longer had to accept the waste. In addition, the community was happy to take down the dam and let the waters flow freely, suggesting the psychological process of letting go of defenses that protect old emotional wounds.

Baia Mare, Romania

There is archeological evidence that gold mining has taken place in the "Golden Quadrilateral" of Transylvania since the Stone Age. The earliest reference to mining in Baia Mare came from Roman settlements in 131 A.D. German migrants continued mining through the Middle Ages until the veins were depleted after the breakup of the Austro-

Hungarian Empire in 1918. Today, mining continues by concession of local citizens.[132] The ore in this area is sulphide-rich, meaning it has a high sulphur content and when exposed to air forms sulphuric acid, which dissolves metals like lead and mercury and thus contaminates groundwater aquifers and drinking water wells.

The mine tailings from the original Roman mines are considered rich when compared with the new ore deposits that are economically viable to mine today. In 1999, an Australian company began reworking mine tailings from these Roman mines, and others, with the goal of extracting more gold from the deposits. They also wanted to remove the "waste" from the environment to more secure tailings dams or cells located away from human populations. The core of the operation included a gold extraction process that used cyanide to form a gold-cyanide complex. An electrolytic process then decomposed the complex, yielding pure gold and destroying the hydrogen cyanide.

In January 2000, this northwestern area of Romania experienced heavy rain that melted a significant snowfall in the mountains. The downpour caused swollen rivers and flooding and caused the tailings dams, where the cyanide extraction was being conducted, to fail. This caused major flooding of cyanide-laden water and sediments onto land and into local rivers. The floodwater that now contained high levels of cyanide and heavy metals entered the Tisza and Danube Rivers and flowed through Romania, Hungary, Yugoslavia, Bulgaria, Moldova, and into the Black Sea.[133] Many fish were killed and several countries' drinking water supplies were contaminated. The incident caused tension between countries and highlighted the necessity of maintaining international environmental standards and safeguards.

I was part of a World Bank team sent to determine the extent of the problem. The team concluded that the responsible culprit was human error in calculating the volume of water that the tailings dams could hold, compared with the strength of the dams. Their calculations had also underestimated the projected volume of rainfall. This is another example of how we are not able to predict the power of nature.

---

132 *Baia Mare, 2008,* on Wikipedia (online).
133 *UNEP, 2000* (online).

As I walked around the flooded area, it looked and felt like the English village I grew up in. The houses reminded me of some I knew in the flood plain of the River Rother in Sussex and induced my empathy for these peoples' lives. However, I noticed a difference in the drinking water wells. These wells were often hand-dug and bricked to prevent cave-ins, or were just wide enough for a bucket to bring up the often dirty water. I found drinking-water wells in farmyards with chickens resting on the top and animals everywhere. Even more striking was that this area felt how I imagined my village would have felt before the Second World War. It had an old-world charm, but it also felt like the people were all waiting for their mother, or government, to take charge and run things for them. In other words, they seemed to be waiting for their environmental problems to be solved by the state, which I saw as a holdover from the Communist era. I felt the grief of their loss of both their water and their innocence. Cyanide had poured into each drinking-water well from the top and bottom, and the contaminant levels were very high. The poison entered at the very heart of their homestead—their drinking water. The people wondered how to deal with the problem because they knew that cyanide is dangerous. Fear and uncertainty lingered everywhere. As the water flowed toward the sea, the anger followed, as did the lawsuits. This was traumatic for the individuals involved, the industry and impacted nations.

This incident highlights the vulnerability of one country at the hands of another. Similar to the issue of global climate change, the unseen releases from one country can greatly impact another. I see the collective moving through similar stages of analysis. That is, the local community and Romanian government had to confront the shadow that emerged in the form of the cyanide flood. Each country was forced to deal with the opposites created by the tension inside and outside of their country and the tension between their own people and the shadow of the spill. They had to deal with the complex of associated feelings around the damage to their own country and others. It awakened an imagination that eventually manifested as a new energy and a new level of consciousness.

The polluting forced people to see that their behavior had been unconscious and impulsive and that there was a need to reconcile and "own" this shadow material that had flowed in through the contained waters.

This particular case study illustrates Nemesis, or "just retribution" in our present-day world. That is, industry has an arrogant disregard for nature and the power that she holds. The Australian company that developed the project in conjunction with the local government grossly miscalculated the volume of water that the tailings dams would hold. This company was so eager to implement their project that they rushed into gold recovery without planning or preparing for all emergencies. Their arrogance in conducting the project led to an overflowing dam. In their "Penthian position" of above and separate, they underestimated the power of nature. Nature's retribution was to wash away the project. The sad part of the story is that local residents held a naive hope that the gold mine operation would clean up the tailings that continued to leach heavy metals into the soil and groundwater around their towns. To add even more confusion and conflict, some of the residents worked at the mine. The company that fed them also caused a permanent change to and destruction of their environment. This situation reminds me of the story of Erysichthon because it is as if nature is saying, "Enough; this land has been exploited for centuries but no more."

The project led to a greater consciousness of nature and how one country's project can impact another's. It raised environmental awareness throughout the entire geographic area. Following the flood, environmental laws were strengthened. However, those most impacted by the damage waged an intense legal campaign against Romania. Financial settlements between the involved countries far exceeded any amount of money that could have come from the mine tailings recovery and Romania saw no benefit from the project in the end. The Nature archetype expressed itself and humans had to come together to respond.

Even though environmental laws have been strengthened, on October 4, 2010, a reservoir holding toxic alumina sludge at the Magyar Aluminium Zrt. Plant ruptured at their plant about 100 miles southwest of Budapest. The reservoir released as much as 700,000 cubic meters (25 million cubic feet) of a bright red sludge. The metals, that cause the red color, and the high pH killed at least four and injured at least 120 people and has devastated the countryside, and impacted farmland and water supplies. The Hungarian government is attempting to prevent the red sludge from polluting the Danube River as the cyanide spill did approximately ten years earlier in Romania.

We could look at these natural and man-made disasters, and our responses to them, as expressions of the Nature archetype. The oil spill in the Gulf comes at a time when American dependence on foreign oil is high and politically unacceptable, driving the need for off-shore oil drilling close to U.S. shores where it is both technically challenging to tap and politically ambivalent. Essentially, environmental groups find it unacceptable and industrial groups argue it is unavoidable.

The question of who is to blame for the BP/Transoceanic disaster and whether criminal negligence was involved is unresolved at this point, but several things are clear. The financial pressures in favor of making immediate decisions appeared to have outweighed a cautious, measured approach to preventing a blowout at a time when the process was at its most vulnerable. Blowout preventers failed or were not replaced, leading to too much gas pressure, which then led to the blowout, a fire, and subsequent loss of life and the drilling platform itself. The uncapped gusher is releasing millions of gallons of oil every day, and the combined resources of one of the most powerful oil companies in the world and the most powerful country in the world are powerless, though patently motivated to staunch the flow. The image of oiled birds is the tip of the iceberg that we are allowed to see. The carcasses of sea life are disposed of each day without witnesses, while the sea creatures that become coated in oil die and fall to the sea floor in their millions, without witnesses, and the already threatened species of the Gulf go unprotected. The U.S. Fish and Wild Life Service has listed thirty-eight species protected by the Endangered Species Act that have been impacted by BP's spill, and the following species are in grave danger: the Bluefin tuna, the Sperm Whale, the Brown Pelican, the Whale Shark and Dolphins.[134] It has been reported that endangered sea turtles were burned with the oil during controlled burns. More: the toxicity of the oil dispersants being used by BP is unknown, but it is believed that they are highly toxic to sea life. How will these creatures ever be replaced?

---

[134] U.S Fish and Wildlife, 2010 (online).

There have been many oil spills since the Industrial Revolution and the development of the internal combustion engine. In the U.S., the most well known is the Exxon Valdiz. The tanker ran aground on Bligh Reef in Prince William Sound and released 10.8 million gallons (25,000 barrels) of oil. The Captain of the Valdiz was found to have been drinking. In his book, *The Fate of Nature,* Charles Wohlforth describes the effects of this oil spill and the subsequent cleanup on the ecology of Prince William Sound and the surrounding area. The spill was similar to the BP spill in the Gulf in that huge numbers of oiled birds, fish and other sea life died. Further, the cleanup process used by Exxon, hot water and detergents, caused further long-term destruction of the environment. The ensuing legal battle between Exxon and the U.S. government, state authorities and local fishing communities caused further devastation to these communities. It appeared that with each legal appeal, fines were reduced and the communities suffered more. It also appeared that many individuals who stood up for the rights of the community suffered too.

However, one interesting factor came out of the process. Community advisory groups were established that allowed for input from the local communities into establishing safety protocols, shipping lanes and other processes that would safeguard sensitive wildlife areas in the future. These groups provided the locals with a voice in the process and limited the power that was given to Exxon officials. The model may be useful for resolving the ongoing issues emerging in the Gulf spill.

In this case, the Prince William Sound Regional Citizens' Advisory Council was formed to "help combat the complacency seen as responsible for the 1989 spill."[135] The council has produced a number of documents illustrating steps taken to provide oversight on the safe transportation of crude oil through Prince William Sound. The Advisory Council has documented many of the findings and experiences related to spill prevention, cleanup and the psychological impacts on local communities.[136]

---

135 Mark Swanson, Prince William Sound Regional Citizens' Advisory Council, Role of Citizen Oversight in the Safe Management of Oil Transportation Operations and Facilities in Prince William Sound, Anchorage, Alaska.
136 John Devens, *Community Versus Big Oil,* 32nd Annual Michigan Conference of Po-

As previously discussed, individual or personal complexes are constellated around environmental issues. These complexes are very strong because they concern basic survival instincts. That is, they activate complexes related to the instinctual pole of the Nature archetype. However, the response to the spill Exxon Valdez spill, the BP-Amoco Refinery cleanup, the Milltown Superfund site, and to many more of these environmental problems, appears to constellate a reaction in the affected communities that brings them together. Working groups are potentially created out of constellate complexes related to problem solving, structured actions oriented towards safety, community, and relationship (albeit related to conflict resolution). These complexes are oriented toward the spiritual pole of the Nature archetype. Referring to Jung's model of the crystal seeding from a solution, the crystal that formed out of the mother liquor of the spill was one oriented towards a community that placed protection of nature high on the priorities of the social order. Using the model of the cultural complex,[13] the layer between the archetypal (Nature archetype) and the personal was activated within a sub-group of the affected community that produced sufficient psychic energy to move the group to community-oriented action.

Further, returning to Kalsched's persecutor/protector complex-model in reference to these case studies, the "complacency" noted as contributing to the Exxon Valdez spill is common to all of the environmental problems, whether it was complacency on the part of the regulating community or industry, or the affected community. Psychologically, speaking out to raise awareness also increases one's visibility, making one a target for projections within the community. As Jung noted, one may attract the projected shadow. In other words, if people speak out too much without support, they are scapegoated or ignored. In order to protect oneself from attack and annihilation by the community, industry or "the other," one tends to become self-prosecutorial, holding one's experience, feeling and personal truth inside. Where the Nature archetype is concerned, our experiences are so deeply embedded, or so deeply rooted in the human psyche, and our internal conflict is often so strong that it is

---

litical Scientists, 2000; see Prince William Sound Regional Citizens' Advisory Council, also website: http://pwsrcac.info/citizen-oversight.

debilitating for us to speak out. This is an effective illustration of the "archetypal defenses of the personal spirit" in action at the level of the group. It is a powerful defense and would explain why we appear incapable of being proactive to prevent many of the problems illustrated in the case studies. Consistent with the analysis of personal trauma-related complexes, a group working in relationship with each other can provide an effective counterweight to the persecutor/protector complex and make changes in favor of nature as illustrated by these examples.

Based on the above myths and case studies, it appears that our individual and collective tendency is to pollute and dump and to overuse a resource; to do the opposite, it seems, is a work against our human nature, or as Jung would call it, an *opus contra naturam*. These oil spills, toxic sludge releases, and global climate change could be seen as part of a process of change, induced as a synchronistic accident by the Nature archetype to bring about greater consciousness. If so, these events may be part of our earth-consciousness evolutionary cycle. Humanity may have to step out of our current paradigm to gain some perspective on our relationship to the Nature archetype and grow more conscious through it.

The following chapter contains an exploration of a selected alchemical text and a twentieth-century love story that is germane to the Nature archetype. The alchemical text is taken from Jung's *Mysterium Coniunctionis* and concerns the idea of *unus mundus*, or One World, which I see as a discussion of the Nature archetype itself. The love story is taken from a novel by J. R. R. Tolkien and represents an image of how we might relate to the Nature archetype. It reveals how to love nature and bring about a different relationship with her and with the archetype that lies underneath nature's many manifestations.

6
Alchemy and the Silmarillion

It is only possible to come to a right understanding and appreciation of a contemporary psychology problem when we can reach a point outside our own time from which to observe it. This point can only be some past epoch that was concerned with the same problems, although under different conditions and in other forms.[137]

Jung became interested in alchemy after reading Herbert Silberer's *Problems of Mysticism and Its Symbolism*.[138] Then, after reading Richard Wilhelm's *The Secret of the Golden Flower*, he re-examined his thoughts on alchemy and acquired the alchemical treatise *Artis auriferae volumina duo*. When he realized that the alchemists spoke in symbols, he started to translate and interpret alchemical texts with the help of his student-assistant (later analyst-colleague) Marie-Louise von Franz.

Jung soon saw that there were two types of alchemical text, one that related to chemistry, and one that was essentially a spiritual process albeit described using chemical terms and metaphors. The alchemy discussed by Jung related to this spiritual form of alchemy. Jung believed these later alchemists were projecting their own spiritual process onto the substances and the reactions they studied:

Investigations of alchemical symbolism, like a preoccupation with mythology, does not lead one away from life any more than a study of comparative anatomy leads away from the anatomy of the living man. On the contrary, alchemy affords us a veritable treasure house of symbols, knowledge of which is extremely helpful for an understanding of neurotic and psychotic processes.[139]

The alchemists described much of their work in terms of nature and natural processes. For example, the rather confusing Axiom of Ostanes

[137] Foreword to "The Psychology of the Transference," *The Practice of Psychotherapy,* CW 16, p. 166.
[138] "The Technique of Differentiation," *Two Essays,* CW 7, par. 360.
[139] Nathan Schwartz-Salant, *Jung on Alchemy,* p. 24.

conveys this keen interest in all aspects of nature: "A nature is delighted by another nature, a nature conquers another nature, a nature dominates another nature."[140] The formula attributed to Democritus shows the same interrelated idea: "Nature rejoices in Nature, Nature conquers Nature, Nature rules over Nature."[141]

Another aspect of the alchemists' work is "the rescue of nature," which has Gnostic roots. The idea of rescuing nature puts the alchemist in the position of the hero, also placing the alchemist above nature. Other aspects of alchemy focus on the *coniunctio,* the conjunction or coming together of the opposites, which is often represented by the joining of masculine and feminine.

Since Jung's work on alchemy, alchemical writings and research are now extensive, so I have limited the discussion here to one allegory that is relevant to this book because of its illustration of the *coniunctio* on the personal and collective levels. It reflects the idea of the *unus mundus* or the One World theory discussed by Jung.[142] In its essence, it is the idea that within the world there is an energy, a life force, or what scientists might call a field, that we are both exposed to and part of. That field affects each of us, and we are aware of this field to the degree to which we have done our own psychological or spiritual work.

The concept is no different from that of magnetism. We are in the earth's magnetic field and are subject to its flux, its changes and effects, but without the appropriate instrument we cannot detect or measure it. Day to day we do not feel it, yet it impacts us. Some are naturally attuned to it. Bernstein suggests that some individuals with trauma are more susceptible to it. He calls it the "Borderland experience," In the following passage, he could also be describing the experience of *unus mundus*:

> However, Borderland experience does not represent either "fantazying" or "genuine imagination." It is not an *intrapsychic* relationship between the ego and the Self. It is *experience.* It is a vis-à-vis *relationship* between the individual and the transrational dimension of reality. Historically, this relationship has been attributed as "magical," i.e., *not real.* But for the Bor-

---

140 Ibid., p. 8.
141 Greg Mogenson, "The Eyes of the Background," in *Spring 75,* pp. 43ff.
142 "The Conjunction," *Mysterium Coniunctionis,* CW 14, pars. 660f.

derland personality it is experience of transrational *reality*. Hannah didn't fantasize or imagine or project the pain of the cows. She felt it. Young children feel these things too – as did the woman above who in first grade experienced insects dying in the sleeping jar."[143]

Bornstein hypotheses that one portal to the Borderland is early childhood trauma.[144] It is not unreasonable to theorize that the connection between the Borderland experience and nature-consciousness operates through *unus mundus*.

The alchemists believed that our connection to nature was both the work (the *opus)* and the goal. Within the context of this book, it is the field of the Nature archetype that affects the human psyche and makes us sensitive to the fate of oiled birds, the disappearing polar bear and, perhaps, the plight of all of the natural world in the age of massive pollution and global climate change.

Gerhard Dorn and *Unus Mundus*

The concept of *unus mundus* came to Jung's attention when he was studying alchemy and specifically the work of Paracelsus and his student Gerhard Dorn. In *Mysterium Coniunctionis* Jung describes how the alchemists imagined their own process of individuation, or personal enlightenment.[145] Marie-Louise von Franz also discusses this same text,[146] noting that the alchemists see three stages in the process of connecting to the greater universe. Here is a simplified overview: In the first stage, the opposites in the psyche would be resolved to become of one mind (no small task). In the second stage, the single mind would be reconciled with the body, and the resulting embodied mind (a Self image) could be linked, in the third stage, with the universal mind and to the One World, the *unus mundus*. Jung explains the third stage further:

> The One and Simple is what Dorn called the *unus mundus*. This "one world" was the *res simplex*. For him the third and highest degree of conjunction was the union of the whole man with the *unus mundus*."[147]

---

[143] Bernstein, Living in the Borderland, pp. 97f.
[144] Ibid., p. 91 (italics in original).
[145] CW14, par. 759.
[146] Alchemical Active Imagination, p. 35.
[147] *"The Conjunction,"Mysterium Coniunctionis,* CW 14, par. 760.

Jung goes on to point out that the *unus mundus* is that state of the "potential world of the first day of creation before the world of multiplicity as we see it." It therefore represents a time, psychologically, before the conscious separation from *participation mystique* or the *ouroboric* state of unconsciousness described by Erich Neumann.[148] In short, *unus mundus* is the One World from which we came and so it is the world that we feel a connection to beyond our conscious knowledge. It is present without being consciously seen. For example, when awareness is lowered to a daydreaming state and the conscious mind is not active, we are more susceptible to the presence of nature. The colors of the world are more intense, and we might see birds and flowers with different eyes. It is shown in the movie *Star Trek Insurrection,* in a scene where a three-hundred-year-old woman (an anima figure who has not physically aged beyond her 40s) is demonstrating how a moment in time is linked to a wider universe. When she holds Jean-Luc Picard's hand (brings him into relationship), the speeding wings of a hummingbird slow down and the seeds from a flower hang suspended in mid-air. The presence of the land and water is felt in a deep way; she has connected Picard to the soul within nature. It is what the Romans called the *genius loci*, the soul of a place. Being connected to it is the felt-sense connection to the One World.

As noted above, the goal of the process of individuation is to conjoin the product of the first stage of the work (the union of opposites which forms the *unio mentalis*) with the body in the second stage. Jung notes that Dorn calls the product of this stage the caelum: "What he called caelum is, as we have seen, a symbolic preconfiguration of the Self."[149] Jung goes on to say that "the caelum also signifies man's likeness to God (Imago Dei), the anima mundi in matter, and the truth itself. It has a thousand names. It is also the Microcosm, the whole man."[150] In other words, if the alchemist (representative of someone seeking individuation) can unite the opposites, resolve inner conflict and embody the experience, then he grasps an aspect of the Self.

---

148 The Origins and History of Consciousness, p. 10.
149 Mysterium Coniunctionis, CW 14, par. 770.
150 Ibid.

Jung explains that the alchemist Dorn "saw the third and highest degree of conjunction in a union or relationship of the adept, who has produced the caelum, with the unus mundus; this would consist, psychologically, in a synthesis of the conscious with the unconscious."[151] Thus, if we imagine this as a dynamic living process with energy flowing between the human ego and the Self, not only could the alchemist resolve opposites within (the ego), but the alchemist could also receive guidance from the Self. As this process became embodied, the alchemist might experience a deeper opening of the mind. If the new embodied consciousness joined with *unus mundus,* then the process became transcendent and the alchemist would have succeeded in joining conscious and unconscious. He/she would be fully connected with the Self at this point. Therefore, *unus mundus* represents what the physicists might call a unified field, a theory that explains all physical properties. But it does not mean going back into *participation mystique,* which would be what Jung termed a "regressive restoration of the persona," as a solution, because the alchemist would have gained a new level of consciousness as a result of the experience, as indeed would we.

Jung wrote to Wolfgang Pauli in October 1953, saying of Dorn:

> For him, the objective of the alchemical opus is, on the one hand, self-knowledge, which is at the same time knowledge of God and on the other hand it is the union of the physical body with the so-called *unio mentalis,* consisting of soul and spirit, which comes about through self-knowledge. From this (third) stage of the opus there emerges, as he states, the unus mundus, the one world, the Platonic prior or primeval world that is also the future of the eternal world.[152]

I suggest that if we apply Jung's and Dorn's alchemical model to our problem of overuse and dumping of waste onto nature, a number of possibilities of a path forward emerge. Using this model, connecting to the *unus mundus* represents the goal for a "future eternal world" or permanent working relationship with nature. This is a process that I believe is, like our personal experience of *unus mundus,* achievable from time to

---

151 Ibid., par. 760.
152 Meier, Atom and Archetype, pp. 128f.

time, but may not be achievable as a permanent state of mind for most of us. The difficulty, of course, is that the process takes place in the unconscious and is accessible only through feeling and imagination. It requires slowing down and lowering our consciousness, similar to the Star Trek movie example mentioned earlier. It is a psychological process of becoming aware. This concept might be too abstract for the general population, particularly one faced with environmental contamination and concerns about health and security, and often operating out of a complex. However, it is essential that we remain open to the imagination and to the Self's influence when we tackle these immense problems. If we can do so according to the alchemical model, then the influence of the Self can flow through us, changing us and those around us.

With this idea of *unus mundus*, we can see that the human psyche is connected (through the personal and collective unconscious) to the world and so to nature. We might experience this connection through feeling tranquility in a certain place, oneness with ourselves in a moment inspired by contact with nature, or through other deep spiritual connections inspired by nature. Such experiences reflect our connection to the Nature archetype. Also, we may imagine this as a dynamic process with energy flowing in both directions. Nature, through the Nature archetype, can express itself through the unconscious in the body and psyche of the individual.

Indeed, Jung has argued, based on his alchemical studies, that our relationship with nature essentially works both ways. That is, nature is so much a part of us that the psyche is connected to nature and its changes. The growing incidents of natural disasters, particularly hurricanes, tornadoes, tidal waves and cyclones, the mounting scientific evidence of global change, particularly species loss, the destruction of coral and more, must influence the psyche. When we hear these stories and see the devastating images on television, we are bound to feel it. Jung would argue that we feel it in our soul and reconnects us to the earth. I am suggesting that although these disasters are emotionally disturbing, they connect us to the Nature archetype.

I believe this unconscious connection to the Nature archetype runs through both the individual and the collective. We often personify the

101

Nature archetype as a natural spirit (an *anima mundi*) or as Gaia (which is a reflection of a desire to return to mother). By consciously understanding both the positive and negative aspects of this connection, we may be better able to allow the Nature archetype to work through us, inspiring a better stewardship of nature.

The Silmarils

The British author J. R. R. Tolkien wrote a series of fantasy books based on a variety of cultural myths. He uses Norse, Icelandic (particularly the Kalavala), and Celtic mythology in his writings. His best-known trilogy is *The Lord of the Rings,* now a major motion picture series. Tolkien tells of a battle with an evil creature called Sauron, who develops machines and genetically engineers a variety of creatures.

Essentially, Sauron represents the industry of Tolkien's time. Simple farming creatures called Hobbits and others, who traditionally face Sauron, represent good. In *The Lord of the Rings,* the Hobbit Frodo agrees to carry and destroy a ring that holds part of Sauron's life force or soul. Once the ring is destroyed, Sauron's reign of power will end. Saruman, one of Sauron's allies, is a wizard who can also make engines of war, conduct genetic engineering, and create selective breeding programs in order to make new races of creatures.

It is obvious that Tolkien respected and revered nature. He saw himself as a Hobbit and his depiction of Saruman is a metaphorical representation of the scientists who transformed Britain during World War Two and later. Ironically, my own educational background as a scientist comes from this era. Often scientists ask, "Can we do something," but fail to ask, *"Should* we do something?" The development of the atomic bomb is a good example. The greatest minds in physics unlocked the secret of the atom and thus released humanity's ability to destroy itself.

The Lord of the Rings can be viewed as a mythic battle between those who are aligned with nature and those who represent a soulless, rapacious, destructive industry. Seen through the lens of Eliade, Tolkien's book is a description of the myth of the Eternal Return. The farming-based Hobbits (archaic humanity/the annual cycles of harvest) are pitted against Sauron and Saruman (the dark aspects of modern industry such as industrial dumping and lack of caring for the earth and natural resources). Also, Tolkien creates a race of ancient talking trees (the Ents) that symbolize the spirit of the forest, which is being destroyed due to industrialization. The story of the Ents reminds us of the myth of Gilgamesh, where men defeat nature in the forest of Lebanon.

In his last book, *The Silmarillion*, published after his death, Tolkien describes the history of the land in which *The Lord of the Rings* is set. He wanted *The Lord of the Rings* and *The Silmarillion* to be published together "as one long saga of the Jewels and the Ring."[153] *The Silmarillion* expands Tolkien's nature-based themes to show additional outcomes in the battle of good versus evil, nature versus industrialization. Tolkien's love for nature comes through in his imaginative books. As a modern metaphor for our relationship with nature, *Silmarillion* provides insights into our current predicament. I have been reading Tolkien since I was sixteen years old and *The Silmarillion* is a rich book that has influenced who I am and how I work. There is one story within the book that has fascinated me since I read it. It is the story of Beren and Lúthien.

To provide some background, the first chapter of *The Silmarillion* is a creation myth where the creator, Eru or the One, also called Iluvatar, creates the world out of his thoughts. He asks the races he creates to make "Great Music" with harmonious themes and it is good to him. Then, "It came into the heart of Melkor to interweave matters of his own imagining that were not in accord with the themes of Iluvatar."[154] As the creation progresses, Melkor, who is evil, plays an increasingly disruptive role in the cycles and rhythms of life (nature). The Elves, one of the races created, are a nature-loving people who tend the trees. Two of their greatest treasures include two "Trees of the Light of Valinor" that are of immense beauty, as a magnificent light emanates from them. One of the Elves, Fëanor, creates three jewels called the Silmarils, hard and strong:

> And the inner fire of the Silmarils Fëanor made of the blended light of the Trees of Valinor, which lives in them yet, though the light of the Trees have long since withered and shine no more.[155]

---

153 C. Tolkien, in J. R. R. Tolkien, *The Silmarillion,* preface to the second edition.
154 Ibid., p. 16.
155 Ibid., p. 67.

Therefore, the jewels can be seen as nature's essence, soul and light. The Trees of Valinor are killed by the unquenchable greed of a giant spider called Ungoliant, a quintessentially negative mother figure. However, that is another story. *The Silmarillion* continues:

> And Varda hallowed the Silmarils, so that thereafter no mortal flesh, nor hands unclean, nor anything of evil will might touch them, but it was scorched and withered: and Mandos foretold that the fates of Arda, earth, sea, and air, lay locked within them.[156]

Therefore, the Silmarils are the essence of nature bound into a jewel, the fate of which is coupled with the fate of the world. This is a metaphor for our earth at this time: the fates of Arda are the fates of humanity because we are bound to nature. Nature gives us everything. The Silmarils also represent the time before our consciousness of nature. They are a symbol of the spirit of the woods and the energy of the *anima mundi*, the animation in all matter,[157] bound into matter.

As the book progresses, Sauron, who is here called Morgoth, the evil servant of Melkor, steals the Silmarils and binds them in a crown of iron. This represents our modern culture where we take nature or the fruits of nature and bind them into machines. For example, oil is pumped from the earth, "tortured" in the refining process, and bound up into metal cars where its power is harnessed. Many of our most precious jewels of nature are now held captive as jewels in the crown of industry and technology. Symbolically, one of our tasks today is to free the Silmarils from the crown, that is, to free nature from the binding oppression of industrial overuse and externalization.

In the tale of Beren and Lúthien (called "The Lay of Leithian"), we see Tolkien's imagination at work on the relationship between mankind (personified in Beren) and nature (an elf named Lúthien). Beren is the son of the chief of one of the great tribes of men and Lúthien is the daughter of the King of the Elves, the race who created the Silmarils. The Elves live in harmony with nature. Lúthien can also be seen as Beren's anima, the feminine goddess of nature, and as a collective anima

---

156 Ibid.

157 "The Conjunction," *Mysterium Coniunctionis,* CW 14, par. 748.

figure, the *anima mundi*. Later in the story, she is even personified as an aspect of the Self. A simple diagram of the story is shown in Figure 5.

At the beginning of the story, the servants of Morgoth kill Beren's father, Barahir (of the house of Finarfin), and cut off his ring hand. The ring is shown in Figure 6 (next page).[158] The ring is an image of *unio mentalis*, where the opposites are reconciled. Like the serpents in alchemy (Figure 7, next page), the ring images the tension of opposites:

> For this ring was like two twin serpents, whose eyes were emeralds, and their heads met beneath a crown of golden flowers, that the one upheld and the other devoured; that was the badge of Finarfin and his house.[159]

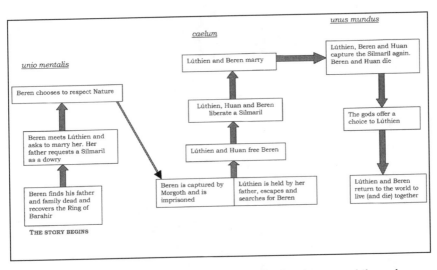

Figure 5. A diagram of "The Lay of Leithian," as interpreted through the goal of *Unus Mundus*.

The ring of Barahir is strikingly similar to an alchemical image of the opposites from an alchemical text (Figure 7). Jung believed that holding the tension of opposites was a key step in the activation of the transcendent function, symbol formation and individuation.

---

158 In *The Lord of the Rings*, the ring of Barahir is owned by Aragon who marries the Elf Arwin.
159 Tolkien, *The Silmarillion*, p. 167.

In Figure 7, the lower serpent represents the lower regions (earth or man) while the winged serpent represents the upper regions (air or heaven). Bearing the ring of Barahir, Beren carries a symbol of the collective union of heaven and earth or his personal union with Lúthien. It is also, therefore, an image of *caelum*. Beren unwittingly goes out hunting and returns to find his family dead. He retrieves the ring from the servants of Morgoth and wanders in grief through Middle Earth until he comes to the land of the Elves. He sees Lúthien dancing and falls in love with her.

Figure 6: The Ring of Barahir.

Figure 7: Eleazar, *Uraltes Chymisches Werk,* Leipzig, 1760.

Like many English men and women after Enclosure, Beren is cut off from his roots, his connection to his family history, and is left with only a ring (a symbol of relationship) for remembrance. While wandering in nature he falls in love with Lúthien (nature), an Elf and daughter of the King of Elves. He asks for her hand in marriage and the King replies, "Bring me in your hand a Silmaril from Morgoth's crown; and then, if she will, Lúthien may put her hand in yours."[160]

This is a challenge for Beren to rescue nature before he can marry Lúthien. As in many fairy tales, the King of Elves challenges Beren to heroic action. Psychologically, the old king represents an out-dated consciousness that must be transformed. Even though he is connected to nature he still embodies, metaphorically, the attitude of a government that continues to do the same thing over and over again and does not have the foresight to seek alternative solutions to the problems predicted twenty-five years earlier. His attitude toward his daughter demonstrates patriarchal rigidity. Here Beren represents the need for a new psychological approach, a leap in consciousness.

The King's challenge becomes a double bind for Beren: go and be killed, or stay in the torment of a love denied. It is Eliade's complex of death or exile, and the challenge felt by a worker in a mining or oil town. Beren decides to leave on his quest. Lúthien's father holds her under house arrest because he knows she will try to find Beren. Lúthien here represents nature being imprisoned by the old king, much like the contemporary Colorado or Alaskan wilderness areas held hostage to oil and gas leases. He can also be seen as a protector/persecutor complex.

When he is in the wild, Beren undergoes a personal change and becomes a vegetarian, foregoing meat. Given the setting of the story, this would make survival quite difficult, yet can be seen as a statement of internal respect for nature. Beren internally resolves the opposites of his human instinctual carnivorous animal roots with his spiritual beliefs and new aspirations. It is a position that might represent *unio mentalis*. I do not suggest that we all become vegetarian, but this choice often represents a recognition that many of our lifestyle choices are in conflict with nature and that we have been unaware of where our food comes from.

---

160 Ibid., p. 167.

Unconsciously, modern society is in denial about the impacts we are having on the earth, and how nature is present in our daily lives. Symbolically, returning to a vegetarian diet is a way of remaining conscious of our relationship with nature and animals.

Unfortunately, Beren and his cousins are captured by the servants of Morgoth and imprisoned. Eventually, Lúthien breaks free of her house arrest and attempts to find Beren, accompanied by Huan, the chief of wolfhounds, a fierce dog. Huan was not born on Middle Earth but instead came from "the beginning of time," which suggests that he is linked to archetypal instincts and is aligned with nature. Together they find Beren in Morgoth's stronghold. When they arrive, Morgoth turns himself into a wolf and tries to defeat Huan, but loses and is forced to free Beren.

Psychologically this represents a joining of spirit (Lúthien) and instinct (Huan) that can free humanity (Beren). Huan symbolizes our instinctual side that knows there is a problem with how we approach nature today. That wolf part of us is ready to fight for change. The spiritual aspect of nature has been imprisoned by an old consciousness and a part of us knows that change is needed. When the spiritual and instinctual parts come together, they free humanity from the stronghold of our present material world. We are ensnared by the things we own and think we need, even when our instincts and spirit tell us we must change our consciousness. Symbolically, it is only when we bring these parts together in the quest to become conscious that we can become free of our old way of being. If the archetype has two poles, one instinctual (Huan) and one spiritual (Lúthien), then the tension of the poles must be held symbolically. If this happens and Beren is able to go free, in that moment a new consciousness can emerge.

In addition to instincts, Huan represents the fangs of nature that can rip into industry and technology. In the same way that Nemesis brings retribution in the form of Famine to Erysichthon, the destruction of oil platforms in the gulf caused by Hurricane Katrina or the massive increase of tornadoes in the Midwest are nature's retribution. Natural disasters can be understood as the Huan energy of our modern world. It is in the interest of industrialized nations to recognize the potential magnitude of damage that can be caused by nature when the wolfhound is set free.

Psychologically, Lúthien's quest for Beren suggests that nature is interested in a partnership with humanity. Perhaps more specifically, nature is interested in trying to enter into the bastions of industry to rescue humanity. This importantly suggests that humanity needs to use nature in order to solve environmental problems. For instance, in hazardous waste cleanup, bacteria are used to clean up oil spills through the process of bioremediation. Wetland ponds are used to clean up mine wastes and trees are used to remove solvents from contaminated aquifers. These examples show how nature is willing to be used in alternative ways to benefit society, just as Lúthien is willing to enter Morgoth's stronghold in order to free Beren.

Morgoth represents industry's need for power and dominance over nature. He becomes a wolf and fights Huan because he wants to keep Beren captive in his stronghold. The wolf is an apt image. It illustrates an abiding regard for defending its territory, and also expresses the shadow aspect of the psyche that is ferocious in its instinctual need for food. This is similar to Erysichthon who also acts like a ravenous wolf. The wolf has been feared for centuries and in "The Lay of Leithian" symbolizes the conflict between instinct and intellect.

After his defeat by Huan, Morgoth raises a wolf of his own called Carcharoth. If Morgoth represents industry, then Carcharoth represents an instinctual response by industry to acquire the raw power of nature. Building higher levies and stronger hurricane-proof buildings or drilling for more oil is the equivalent of breeding Carcharoth. On an animal level, these actions indicate a response that precludes confronting deeper issues, such as working with nature in a collaborative process rather than an adversarial one.

After Lúthien and Huan free Beren, he is healed in nature. Eventually Beren decides to return to complete the quest for the Silmaril. Lúthien and Huan join him, and together they attempt to liberate a Silmaril from Morgoth's crown. Each of the heroes brings special talents to the quest: Lúthien has a voice that mesmerizes Morgoth; Huan has cunning and stealth; and Beren has a knife that will cut the iron of Morgoth's crown. All three bring courage and, most importantly, imagination and confidence that they can complete the task. This suggests that nature can be liberated with a clear voice, imagination, stealth, and discernment (the knife). The words may quiet and calm the hounds of industry and help it to connect to something inside of itself, and imagination will hold the possibility of change. Beren and Lúthien get to the crown and free a single Silmaril, but as they attempt to cut out a second gem, Morgoth suddenly awakes and the two heroes must escape quickly.

In our modern world, trying to get a second Silmaril suggests that overreaching our ability to bring about change is likely to wake the sleeping giant. In psychological terms, when working with a power complex we need to stay conscious of what is constellated. If we move too quickly, the complex reacts with power and fights back, thus solidifying its position. The complex would stimulate a response from industry, especially if industry believes it might be losing what it has gained. Again, we can consider the self-care system that becomes ferociously protective of its position, resisting any relational process.

Lúthien is immortal. In Jungian terms she is an anima figure linked to the Self, Jung's concept of the God within, and represents wholeness. Lúthien and Beren are reunited and successfully take a Silmaril from Morgoth's crown, symbolizing the joining of humanity with instinct and the essence of nature. However, the moment cannot be sustained. It brings about the instinctual opposite, the wolf Carcharoth, who meets them on the bridge, the point of transition between the stronghold and the world. When Beren holds up the Silmaril to frighten Carcharoth, the wolf bites off and swallows Beren's hand and the Silmaril, and then runs in pain and terror with these new contents in its stomach. Beren and Lúthien escape with the help of Huan who summons three eagles.

Again Lúthien heals Beren, again showing the healing power of nature. They go before Lúthien's father and Beren says, "My quest is fulfilled, even now I have a Silmaril in my hand,"[161] as he shows the arm where the hand is missing. Beren explains that the hand with the Silmaril is in the stomach of Carcharoth. Lúthien's father finally allows the two to marry. Once again they set out to find the Silmaril, but this time Carcharoth is their quarry. When they find the wolf, he has been driven mad by the Silmaril in his stomach and fights furiously. Carcharoth mortally

---

[161] Tolkien, *The Silmarillion,* p. 148.

wounds Beren in the fight before Huan can kill him. However, Huan is also fatally wounded and dies in the process.

The story implies that there is a personal cost to restoring nature. It may take acts of individual heroism to change the earth's present course. Most notably, it takes sacrifice and courage to challenge the "wolf of industry." In the Exxon Valdiz example discussed earlier, Exxon, like Morgoth, was a nonhuman foe. Wohlforth writes:

> Exxon absorbed the hatred of a generation of coastal Alaskans without flinching, impassive, because it is not a person—it is a thing, ultimately just a set of symbols, an interchangeable subsystem in an economic machine that functions without regard to individual's wishes. [162]

I have seen these acts of bravery at public meetings, where individuals are willing to take a stand, even though the collective may sacrifice them. I have attended public meetings in town halls where there may be hundreds of supporters for a particular cleanup project proposed by the responsible party. The cleanup would mean short-term financial income for the town, yet the proposal did not restore the true nature of the damaged area. The original sense of place was not restored, and a few individuals opposed simply giving in to the responsible party.

For most of us it is hard enough to stand in front of several hundred people and say anything. But to stand up in front of a hostile crowd and say no to a proposition that would lead to income and jobs is even more difficult.

Tragically, after the Exxon Valdez spill, a former Mayor of the town of Cordova, committed suicide partly because of the loss of his business and partly because he could not do more to help the town. Rick Steiner, an activist who initially mediated between fishermen and oil company officials, was later rejected by the town and became isolated, impoverished and depressed. Others commented that Rick had been the recipient of vicious comments. Eventually Rick left Cordova. These individual human tragedies express the pathos also inherent within the cultural complex in the face of environmental challenges and disasters. They are the human face of the dilemma between death or exile. Such experiences

---

162 The Fate of Nature: Rediscovering Our Ability to Rescue the Earth, p. 285.

can diminish the individual human spirit to the point of exclusion, isolation and even death.

Another example is the Gulf oil spill. Many people are looking for work and are hired by BP to clean the oil from the beaches. They are required to bear witness to the death and destruction first-hand and see the degradation of their environment. The legal and social pressures are to keep quiet about the experience, but overcoming the psyche's self-care system requires speaking out and sharing the traumatic nature of the events. Locals make psychic and physical sacrifices in order to maintain a good lifestyle, yet have to recognize their collusion with big business over the years. They are now faced with the loss of their innocence and struggle to persevere and retain the jewels (or Silmarils) of their community and personal bonds to each other. I have seen this conflict of community versus personal over and over throughout the years of hazardous waste spills and cleanups.

In Tolkien's story, at the point where the Silmaril is liberated, Lúthien, Beren, Huan and the Silmaril are together in nature. Even though Beren and Huan are mortally wounded, the quest is achieved. Using Figure 5 as a guide, this represents a point of *unus mundus* where the essence of nature (Huan) is present with humanity (Beren) and an aspect of the Self (Lúthien). In this story, it comes at the point of death. However, this can be interpreted as a point of ego-death where the old ego or consciousness dies and a new consciousness emerges, as shown by the case examples. One could say that the goal of *unus mundus* is to integrate the whole person into the essence of nature, or the essence of nature into the whole person. That is to say, when we are consciously engaged with nature around us, we feel the presence of the Nature archetype within us.

However, the story does not end on that note. When Beren dies, "the spirit of Lúthien falls into darkness and her body lay like a flower that is suddenly cut off."[163] She goes to the Hall of Valar (similar to Valhalla, abode of the Norse gods) and she is given a choice: to dwell with the Valar until the world's end or return to Middle Earth with Beren and sacrifice her immortal life. She chooses Beren. This shows how the Nature archetype is brought into relationship and then humanized.

---

[163] Ibid., p. 148.

We can see that psychologically the Hall of Valar is a location out of space and time, where the gods or archetypes dwell, and so represents the Self. It is unknown and unending. When Lúthien returns to the Hall of Valar, she is brought into relationship with the Self. As an archetypal energy, Lúthien represents the spirit of nature returning to the Self before leaving again to rejoin the human realm. Her movement suggests she is a psychopomp, or link between the Self (the Valar) and the ego (the protagonist, Beren). In returning to Beren, Lúthien chooses a mortal life, which suggests that the Self, through the spirit of nature, is present in humanity's relationship with nature.

The story suggests that we integrate the spirit of nature. This sounds simple, but how do we achieve it today? We cannot return to unconscious innocence *(participation mystique)* concerning nature, but must move into a relationship with, and not over, nature. One way of viewing this is using one year of sunlight for one year of the earth's needs, and adjusting our population and earthly requirements to fit with the sunlight we receive. In effect, this is what natural disasters accomplish. However, it is a brutal and nasty process

It also means restructuring our economy to support sustainable growth, as defined by the earth and not just by industry and bankers. A correction is needed to bring the earth's resources back into the equation.

The underlying message of the story is the relationship between the nature spirit (Lúthien) and her human lover, which suggests a symbolic recovery of the essence of nature from the hands of industry.

A simple love of nature is not enough, although it is a good start. We re required to take action. We do not need to adopt Beren's heroic attitude and launch a frontal attack on industry. We can each work to become conscious of our relationship with nature on a daily basis: recycling, choosing recycled products, installing solar panels, choosing green products,, driving less and even picking up trash. Becoming conscious of our relationship to nature also includes how we view each other as human beings who live in nature and at the same time contain nature within; how we relate to each other and how we connect to our own inner place of deep knowing then becomes a highly treasured pursuit.

7
In Conclusion

The integration of personal psychic phenomena with the corresponding transpersonal symbols is of paramount importance for the future development of consciousness and for the synthesis of the personality.[164]

The scientist in me cannot end on such an esoteric note. There is no doubt that the earth is changing due to hazardous waste and global climate effects. Humanity is slowly adjusting its psychology to deal with, adapt to, and integrate these changes. If we do not come to terms with the scientific reality that we have impacted the earth, then we are unlikely to overcome the significant barriers to psychological adjustments. Some of the greatest problems are tribalism, patriarchal religions that promote the oppression of women, large families that add to overpopulation, and a failure to support worldwide renewable (wind and solar) energy solutions, coupled with early education on environmental damage and stewardship. Many segments of the developing world are caught in the shadows of poverty, disease and hunger. They instinctively repeat old patterns of overusing a resource and dumping their household waste locally. That is, they do not have sufficient resources to change this pattern.

In developed countries, individual or corporate greed for high profits has dominated over the long-term view of investing in renewable energy technologies. For example, an oil company can go to the bank and receive a loan for oil development at the prime interest rate. The same loan for solar or wind-powered technologies is prime plus five to ten percent.[165] This illustrates the banking industry's historical reluctance to change its view. The development of a sustainable lifestyle could preserve the planet without dependence on fossil fuels.

---

[164] Neumann, *The Origins*, p. xxiii.
[165] Stephan Noé, of Citizens for a Better Environment, an attorney developing solar power in the Midwest; personal communication.

Jungian archetypal theories provide a good framework for understanding why it is hard to bring about the psychological changes required to alter human behavior in favor of the environment. In the psychological consulting room, change occurs in individuals, but when we are confronted with overwhelming environmental trauma, especially those beyond our personal control, we tend to close down, split off and employ archetypal defenses to prevent the tragedy from affecting the inner person who instinctively loves nature.

However, having worked with trauma, personal and environmental, I believe the process of change can be initiated and the outcome can look different from that predicted by many scientific scenarios. Jungian psychology provides important tools and insights to healing. The work starts with understanding the shadow and how we banish unpleasant or unwanted psychological material to the unconscious, and then values the process of restoring this material back to consciousness. Concerning the environment, working with shadow involves examining our own personal and collective environmental dependencies and excesses. Change often starts small. Personal choice and action are the first steps to change, like the addict who admits dependency as the first step to recovery.

The Nature archetype is a life-force energy flowing into the human psyche through the Self. I am suggesting that the goal of this archetype is to bring humanity into a deeper personal relationship with nature and the earth. Environmental problems serve as opportunities to bring consciousness to our human condition. If we become more conscious and make changes internally and locally, the results can have a global impact.

For example, many towns and cities have the ability to set regulations that require companies to comply with environmental reporting and set chemical release standards or recycling goals. Local companies typically find it easier to respond. Larger companies may find they have multiple requirements for multiple towns or cities, and multinational organizations often find compliance a nightmare. They will push back at the state level through lobbying. State politicians must now listen to local concerns when balancing the pressure from large companies with the rights and needs of their constituents. Therefore, local changes can have far-reaching impacts.

If we look at myths, we see how they illustrate the actions of unconscious people who act out of self-interest and greed. Psychologically, these myths depict an unconscious, unrelated, narcissistic attitude, which is demonstrated in the early history of modern industrial development. Science, technology and the Industrial Revolution did bring about changes, positive and negative, but there was little or no consideration given to the wastes generated in the process, nor the value of nature. Historically, the economic gain for dumping wastes was too great and no thought was given to the relationship between the act of dumping and changes in the environment. The individuals and companies behind the externalization of wastes were acting out of unconscious instinctual drives to dominate or protect themselves from the anxiety caused by fear of poverty. These behaviors now place all of us at risk. Through the courage of individuals who push for a more related approach to nature, we are beginning to see some changes in attitude. This ultimately involves engaging the personal imagination with a commitment to protect nature.

By considering alchemical models and literary analogies that illustrate humanity's relationship with nature and the Nature archetype, we can become conscious of our shadow and personal and collective complexes. Through this process, we will have a more respectful relationship with nature. Consequently, the Nature archetype is creating a powerful change in human consciousness. Thanks to the writings of the alchemist Dorn, we can metaphorically illustrate that humanity is linked to a broader universe through the *unus mundus*, which provides a felt-sense of our world. As shown in Figure 4, nature is all around us as the earth, the solar system and the universe. Psychologically, the Nature archetype was present as human consciousness developed over time. Therefore, our connection to a greater universe through the collective unconscious is challenging twenty-first century humanity to raise its collective consciousness and recognize our relationship with nature as *primary*. This change in consciousness is essential if we are to survive and evolve.

The Nature archetype is linked to the creation of all things and can be seen as an aspect of the *Imago Dei,* the Divine. As Figure 4 depicts, the Nature archetype rises into human consciousness from an origin deep in time and space (the universe) and continues to exert an influence today. Through the alchemical model, it is apparent that the concept of *unus mundus*, a personal body-centered-feeling relationship with nature or the Nature archetype, connects humanity to the Divine on a deep level.

Perhaps through *unus mundus,* we will come to change our personal relationship with nature on a daily basis, such as our relationship to food, transportation and energy. Our adaptation to the future will require such an evolution in personal attitude.

Also consistent with Jungian psychology is the necessity to recognize those nature-traumas that constellate complexes. For example, when listening to a story about natural damages do you "check out" because you do not want to hear the gory details? Are you only likely to get involved if the environmental problem is in your own back yard? If so, can you recognize your own feeling and actions at the time? Also, when you hear about damage to the environment, do you discuss it with your friends or keep it to yourself?

We are unable to know the will of the Divine, or the direction of the Nature archetype, but it is clear that the earth is experiencing pressure through global warming, species loss and environmental disease. Seriously rethinking our relationship to the earth is a psychological and spiritual process that cannot wait.

Now, in the summer of 2010, with the gulf coast already monumentally scarred by the recent oil spill, there is still no reliable estimate of the eventual damage to the environment.

BIBLIOGRAPHY

Aristotle, *Politics,* Book II, Chapter III, 1261b. Trans. Benjamin Jewett as *The Politics of Aristotle: Translated into English with Introduction, Marginal Analysis, Essays, Notes and Indices.* Oxford, UK: Clarendon Press, 1885.

Beek, B. *Bioaccumulation: New aspects and Developments.* New York: Springer Verlag, 2000.

Bernstein, J.S. *Living in the Borderland: The Evolution of Consciousness and the Challenge of Healing Trauma.* New York: Routledge, 2006.

Biedermann, H. *Dictionary of Symbolism, Culture Icons & the Meanings Behind Them.* New York: Facts on File, 1994.

Bolin, I. *Rituals of Respect: The Secret of Survival in the High Peruvian Andes.* Austin, TX: University of Texas Press, 1998.

Byalko, A. *Nuclear Waste Disposal: Geophysical Safety,* vol. 1. Boca Raton, FL: CRC Press Inc., 1994.

Carson, Rachel. *Silent Spring.* New York: Houghton Mifflin, 1962.

CERCLA. *Comprehensive Environmental Response, Compensation and Liability Act,* Title 42, The Public Health and Welfare, Chapter 103, 1980.

CFR, 1998. *Code of Federal Regulations,* vol. 63, (248), 71542-71568.

Crichton, Michael. *State of Fear.* New York: Harper Collins, 2005.

Crossley-Holland, K. *The Norse Myths.* New York: Pantheon Books, 1980.

Devens, J. *Community Versus Big Oil.* 32nd Annual Conference of Political Scientists, 2000.

Dieckmann, Hans. *Complexes.* Berlin: Springer Verlag, 1996.

Du Nunn Winter, D., and Koger, S. *The Psychology of Environmental Problems.* Mahwah, NJ: Lawrence Erlbaum Associates, 2004.

Eliade, Mircia.*The Myth of the Eternal Return, or Cosmos and History.* Princeton: Princeton University Press, 1954.

Ellenberger, H. *The Discovery of the Unconscious.* New York: Basic Books, 1970.

EPA, 1987. *Ecological Risk Assessment Guidance for Superfund, Process for Designing and Conducting Ecological Risk Assessments,* Office of Solid Waste and Emergency Response, Environmental Protection Agency, EPA 540 –R-97-006, June, 1987.

EPA, 1989. *Risk Assessment Guidance for Superfund, vol. I, Human Health Evaluation Manual,* Office of Emergency and Remedial Response, Environmental Protection Agency, EPA/540/1-89/002, December 1989.

EPA, 1999. *Review of the EPA's Proposed Environmental Endocrine Disruptor Screening Program,* EPA-SAB-EC-99-013.

Gardiner, S., Carney, S., Jameson, D., and Shue, H. *Climate Ethics: Essential Reading.* New York: Oxford University Press, 2010.

Grant, M., and Hazel, J. *Who's Who in Classical Mythology*. New York: Routledge, 2002.

Griffin, Susan. *Woman and Nature: The Roaring Inside Her*. New York: Harper and Row, 1978.

Hannah, Barbara. *Jung: His Life and Work, a Biographical Memoir*. Boston: Shambhala, 1991.

Hardin, Garrett. "The Tragedy of the Commons," In *Science*, vol. 162, no. 3859 (1968), pp. 1243-1248.

Harr, Jonathan. *A Civil Action*. New York: First Vintage Books, Random House, 1995.

Heidel, Alexander. *The Gilgamesh Epic and Old Testament Parallels*. 2nd edition. Chicago: Chicago University Press, 1949.

Hill, Julia. *The Legacy of Luna: The Story of a Tree, a Woman and the Struggle to save the Redwood*. San Francisco: Harper Collins, 2000.

Hillman, James. "The Return of the Soul of the World.: In *Spring 1982*.

Hoskins, W.G. *The Making of an English Landscape*. London, UK: Hodder and Stoughton Limited, 1955.

Houghton, J. *Global Warming*. New York: Cambridge University Press, 2004.

Hudson, P. *The Industrial Revolution*. New York: Oxford University Press, 1992.

Humphries, R. *Ovid: Metamorphoses*. Bloomington, IN: Indiana University Press, 1969.

Jacobi, Jolande. *The Psychology of C.G. Jung*. New Haven, CT: Yale University Press, 1973.

Jung, C. G. *C. G. Jung Speaking*. Ed. W. McGuire and R. F. C. Hull. Princeton: Princeton University Press, 1977.

_____. *Collected Papers on Analytical Psychology*. New York: Moffat Yard and Company, 1917.

_____. *The Collected Works* (Bollingen Series XX). 20 vols. Trans. R.F.C. Hull. Ed. H. Read, M. Fordham, G. Adler, Wm. McGuire. Princeton: Princeton University Press, 1953-1979.

_____. *Letters,* vol. 2, 1951-1961. (Bolligen Series XCV-2). Princeton: Princeton University Press, 1953-1975.

_____. *Psychology of the Unconscious Processes*. Collected Papers on Analytical Psychology, 2nd edition. New York: Moffat, Yard and Company, 1917.

Kalsched, Donald. *The Inner World of Trauma: Archetypal Defenses of the Personal Spirit*. New York: Routledge, 1996.

Kerényi, Karl. *Gods of the Greeks*. London, UK: Thames and Hudson, 1960.

Kluger, Rivkah Scharf. *The Archetypal Significance of Gilgamesh*. Einsiedeln, Switzerland: Daimon Verlag, 1991.

Knox, J. *Archetype, Attachment, Analysis*. Routledge, 2003.

Leakey, R. and Lewin, R. *The Sixth Extinction*. New York: Anchor Books, 1995.

Liddick, D. *Ecoterrorism: Radical Environmental and Animal Liberation Movements*. Westport, CT: Praeger Publishers, 2006.

Lloyd W. F. *Two Lectures on the Checks to Population.* Oxford, UK: Oxford University Press, 1833.

Lovelock, J. E. and Margulis, L. "Atmospheric homeostasis by and for the biosphere—The Gaia Hypothesis" *Tellus,* vol. 26, no. 1 (1974).

Lovelock, J. *The Revenge of Gaia.* New York: Basic Books, 2006.

Lovelock, J. *The Age of Gaia.* New York: W.W. Norton, 1988.

MacDermot, V. *The Fall of Sophia.* Great Barrington, MA: Lindisfarne Books, 2001.

Mach, J. "Inventing a Psychology of Our Relationship with the Earth." In S. Staub & P. Green, eds., *Psychology and Social Responsibility.* New York: New York University Press, 1992.

Macy, J. "Working Through Environmental Despair," in T. Roszak, *Ecopsychology.* San Francisco: Sierra Club Books, 1995.

Mair, A. W. *Callimachus Hymns and Epigrams.* Cambridge, MA: Harvard University Press, 1955.

Meeker, J. W. *The Comedy of Survival: Literary Ecology and a Play Ethic.* 3rd edition. Tucson, AZ: University of Arizona Press, 1997.

Meier, C.A. *Atom and Archetype: The Pauli/Jung Letters.* Princeton: Princeton University Press, 2001.

Metzle, Manfred. *Endocrine Disruptors,* part I. New York: Springer-Verlag, 2001.

Mogenson, Greg. "The Eyes of the Background." In *Spring 75,* 2006.

Naess, A., and Rothenberg, D. *Ecology, Community and Lifestyle: Outline of an Ecosophy,* New York: Cambridge University Press, 1990.

NCP, 1980. Title 40--Protection of Environment, Chapter I—EPA, Part 300—National Oil and Hazardous Pollution Contingency Plan, 1980.

Neeson, J. M. *Commoners: Common Rights, Enclosure and Social Change in England, 1700-1820.* New York: Cambridge Univesity Prss, 1993.

Neumann, Erich. *The Great Mother.* (Bollinger Series XLII). 2nd edition. Princeton: Princeton University Press, 1963.

_____. *The Origins and History of Consciousness* (Bollinger Series XLII). Princeton: Princeton University Press, 1954.

National Research Council. *Improving Risk Communication.* Washington, DC: National Academy of Sciences, 1989.

Oxford English Dictionary. Compact edition. London: Book Club Associates, 1979.

Rowland, Susan. "Nature Writing; Jung's Ecologic in the Coniunctio of Comedy and Tragedy." In *Spring 75,* pp. 275-297, 2006.

Ross, S. *The Industrial Revolution.* London: Evans Brothers Limited, 2008.

Roszac, Theodore. *The Voice of the Earth, an Exploration of Ecopsychology.* New York: Simon and Schuster, 1992.

Schwartz-Salant, Nathan. *Jung on Alchemy.* Princeton: Princeton University Press, 1995.

Schneider, S. *Global Warming.* San Francisco: Sierra Club Books, 1989.

Schoen, D. *Divine Tempest: The Hurricane as a Psychic Phenomenon.* Toronto: Inner City Books, 1998.

Serdyuk, I., Zaccai, J., and Zacchia, J. *Methods in Molecular Biophysics: Structure Dynamics and Function.* New York: Cambridge University Press, 2007.

Singer, T., and KImbles, S. L. *The Cultural Complex: Contemporary Jungian Perspective on Psyche and Society.* New York, Routledge, 2004.

Slater, P. *The Glory of Hera: Greek Mythology and the Greek Family.* Boston: Beacon Press, 1968.

Smith, R., trans. *Martin Buber: I and Thou.* New York: Scribner Classics, 2000.

Snurluson, Snorri. *The Prose Edda.* New York: Penguin Classics, 2005.

Sparks, J. Gary. *At the Heart of Matter: Synchronicity and Jung's Spiritual Testament.* Toronto: Inner City Books, 2007.

Stein, Murray. *The Principles of Individuation.* Wilmette, IL: Chiron Press, 2006.

Stevens, A. Archetype Revisited: An Updated Natural History of the Self. *Toronto: Inner City Books, 2003.*

Swanson, M. *Prince William Sound Regional Citizens' Advisory Council: Role of Citizen Oversight in the Safe Management of Oil Transportations Operations and Facilities in Prince William Sound.* Anchorage, Alaska, 2010.

Thucydides, *History of the Peloponnesian War,* Book I, Sec. 141. Trans. Richard Crawley. New York: E. P. Dutton & Co., 1910.

Tolkien, C. *The Silmarillion,* Preface to the Second Edition. New York: Harper Collins, 1999.

Tolkien, J. R. R. *The Hobbit.* New York: Houghton Mifflin, 1937.

_____. *The Lord of the Rings.* London, UK: Allen and Unwin, 1969.

_____. *The Silmarillion.* New York: Harper Collins, 1977.

Von Franz, Marie-Louise. *Creation Myths.* Zurich, Switzerland: Spring Publications 1972.

_____. *Alchemical Active Imagination,* Boston, MA: Shambhala Press, 1997.

Whyte, David. *River Flow.* Langley, WA: Many Rivers Press, 2007.

Wilhelm, Richard. *The Secret of the Golden Flower.* Orlando, FL: Harcourt Brace & Company, 1962.

Wohlforth, C. *The Fate of Nature: Rediscovering Our Ability to Rescue the Earth.* New York: Saint Martins Press, 2010.

Wright, R. *A Short History of Progress.* New York: Carroll & Graf, 2005.

INTERNET SOURCES

Baia Mare, 2008. http://en.wikipedia.org/wiki/Baia_Mare.

Bodiam, 2008. http://en.wikipedia.org/wiki/Bodiam.

Casper 2005. http://www.astswmo.org/files/meetings/2005
BrownfieldsSymposium /BP%20Amoco%20Site%20Casper%20WY.pdf.

Chalquist, Craig. *A Glossary of Jungian Terms. 2008.*
http://www.terrapsych.com/jungdefs.html.

EPA, 2008. *The Milltown Superfund Site, Update,*
http://www.epa.gov/region8/superfund/mt/milltown/

Glossary, 2008. http://www.terrapsych.com/jungdefs.html.

Hillman, James. *On the Anima Mundi*, IDEAA, Instituto de Ecologia Aplicada,
http://www.ideaa.es/wp/?p=765.

New York Times, 2008a
http://www.nytimes.com/interactive/2007/08/26/world/asia/choking_on_growth.html.

New York Times, 2008b.
www.nytimes.com/2008/05/27/science/27dam.html?n=Top/Reference/Times%20Topi
cs/People/R/Robbins,%20Jim

*Peak oil, 2006.*http://www.peak-oil-news.info/military-oil-usage-statistics/

Prince William Sound Regional Citizens' Advisory Council. (Website: http://
pwsreac.info/citizen-oversight.)

UNEP, 2000.   http://www.rec.org/REC/Publications/CyanideSpill/ENGCyanide.pdf

US Fish and Wildlife, 2010. http://www.fws.gov/home/dhoilspill.

Wetlands 2006.
http://www.wbcsd.org/plugins/DocSearch/details.asp?MenuId=MjIx&ClickMe
nu=LeftMenu&doOpen=1&type=DocDet&ObjectId=MTk3MDY.

Wyoming 2008.   http://deq.state.wy.us/volremedi/history.asp.

Index

entries in *italics* refer to illustrations

124

on *unus mundus*, 99
word association experiment, 29
on World Soul, 36

Kalsched, Donald, 13, 73-74, 94
Kerényi, K.: *The Gods of the Greeks*, 57
Kimbles, Samuel: *The Cultural Complex*, 78
king, 107
Kootenai tribe, 45
Kyoto Accord, 39

Levy-Bruhl, Lucien, 12
Lovelock and Margulis, 40
Lowell, Massachusetts, 79-80
Luthien, 104, 106-110, 112-113

Magyar Aluminium Zrt., 91
Manifest Destiny, 68
Manufactured Gas, 79
masculine, 30, 36-37, 47-48, 50
Milltown, Montana, 86-88
Mother Earth, 15-16, 34, 58
Mother, Great, 30, *31*, 35-36, 49-51
mythology/myths, 50, 115
creation, 8, 17-18, 46-47, 61

natural disasters, 48, 101, 108-109, 113
nature, 11-17, 22-26, 30, 35-36, 38-39, 41, 46, 48-49, 56-57, 60-63, 77, 79, 79, 83, 85, 89, 91, 99-101, 104, 107, 109-113, 115-117
consciousness, 19
defined, 10
deprivation, 75
divinities, 43
dominance over, 18, 50, 52-53, 56, 109
Jung on, 16, 35-36
as mother, 16
rescue of, 97
trauma, 74
Nature archetype, 8, 10-12, 14-15, 17, 25, 28-30, 34-38, 41, 43-46, 55, 59, 62, 75, 77-78, 83, 85, 88, 91-92, 94-95, 98, 101, 112-113, 115-117
Nemesis/nemesis, 57, 91, 108

Neumann, Erich, 30-31, 36, 46-47, 99
The Great Mother, 35
neuroscience, 12
non-technological societies, 44
Norse creation myth, 49-50
numinosity/numinous, 11
oil, 54-55, 104
spill(s), 93-94, 112, 117
One World, 11, 17, 97, 99. *See also* unus mundus
opposite(s), 20, 59, 77-78, 90, 99-100, 105, 107
"Other," 19, 46, 71
Ouranos, 47
overpopulation, 16, 41, 115

Pauli, Wolfgang, 100
participation mystique, 12, 24, 43, 46, 99-100, 113
Peloponnesian War, 54
Pentheus/Penthian, 58-60, 91
persecutor/protector complex, 73-75, 94-95, 107
pollution, 8, 13-14, 17, 19, 30, 39, 55-56, 69, 72, 95, 98
power complex, 17
projection, 39
psyche, 38
Jung on, 26-28
structure of, *27,*
psychoanalysis, 39-40. *See also* analysis
psychoid layer, 34, 38
psychological/psychology, 13, 27. See also *Jung, C. G./Jungian*
defenses, 12-13, 71-74, 76, 82, 88, 94, 115
of environmental problems, 70-71

Ragnarok, 49-50
regulations, environmental, 69-70, 82
religions/religious, 11, 47
renewable energy, 114
repetition, 61-62
rescue of nature, 97
retribution, 57, 108. *See also* Nemesis
Ring of Barahir, 105, *106,* 107
risk, assessment, 81-82

communication, 82-83, 87
River Runs Through It, A, 87-88
Roszak, Theodore, *The Voice of the Earth,* 40
Rowland, Susan, 37

Sauron, 102
science/scientist, 19, 56, 73, 102, 114-116. *See also* genetic research.
fiction, 20
Schwartz-Salant, Nathan: *Jung on Alchemy,* 96-97
Self, 11, 17, 19-20, 28-29, 35-36, 43, 45, 48, 77-79, 98-101, 105, 110, 112-113, 115
self-care system, 73-75, 110, 112
separation, 47-48, 63
shadow, 13, 15, 17, 30, 39-40, 53, 56, 83, 85, 90-91, 94, 109, 115-116
collective, 17, 39
Silmarillion, The, 20, 103-105, 107-113
Singer, Thomas and Samuel Kimbles: *The Cultural Complex,* 74-75
Sophia, 36
spectrum, 34
spirit/spiritual, 34, 36, 45, 108
St. Augustine, 32
Star Trek Insurrection, 99
Stevens, Anthony: *Archetype Revisited,* 27
structure of the psyche, *27,*
Superfund, 68, 79-83, 86
Sussex, 22
sustainable, definition of, 113
symbol(s), 18
synchronicity, 38

Thucydides: *History of the Peloponnesian War,* 65
Tolkien, J. R. R., 102-103
"The Lay of Leithian," 104
The Lord of the Rings, 102-103
*The Silmarillion/*Silmarils, 20, 103-105, 107-113
trauma, nature, 74
tree, 49, 53-55
world, *see* Yggdrasil

unconscious, 38, 46, 50, 100
collective, 28, 32, 34, 38, 43, 116
ecological, 72
unified biological system, 41
unified field, 100
unus mundus, 11, 17, 23, 38, 97, 99-101, 112, 116-117

vegetarian, 107-108
Von Franz, Marie-Louise.: *Creation Myths,* 46

waste(s), 66-69, 80, 116. *See also* dumping; externalization
Wohlforth, C.: *The Fate of Nature,* 111
wolf, 109
word association experiment, 29
World Soul, 36-37
world tree, 49
Wright, R.: *A Short History of Progress,* 42-43

Yggdrasil, 49

Also in this Series, by James Hollis

THE MIDDLE PASSAGE: From Misery to Meaning in Midlife
ISBN 0-919123-60-0. (1993) 128pp. *Sewn* $25
Why do so many go through so much disruption in their middle years? Why then? What does it mean and how can we survive it? Hollis shows how we can pass through midlife consciously, rendering the second half of life all the richer and more meaningful.

UNDER SATURN'S SHADOW: The Wounding and Healing of Men
ISBN 0-919123-64-3. (1994) 144pp. *Sewn* $25
Saturn was the Roman god who ate his children to stop them from usurping his power. Men have been psychologically and spiritually wounded by this legacy. Hollis offers a new perspective on the secrets men carry in their hearts, and how they may be healed.

TRACKING THE GODS: The Place of Myth in Modern Life
ISBN 0-919123-69-4. (1995) 160pp. *Sewn* $25
Whatever our religious background or personal psychology, a greater intimacy with myth provides a vital link with meaning. Here Hollis explains why a connection with our mythic roots is crucial for us as individuals and as responsible citizens.

SWAMPLANDS OF THE SOUL: New Life in Dismal Places
ISBN 0-919123-74-0. (1996) 160pp. *Sewn* $25
Much of our time on earth we are lost in the quicksands of guilt, anxiety, betrayal, grief, doubt, loss, loneliness, despair, anger, obsessions, addictions, depression and the like. Perhaps the goal of life is not happiness but meaning. Hollis illuminates the way.

THE EDEN PROJECT: In Search of the Magical Other
ISBN 0-919123-80-5. (1998) 160pp. *Sewn* $25
A timely and thought-provoking corrective to the fantasies about relationships that permeate Western culture. Here is a challenge to greater personal responsibility—a call for individual growth as opposed to seeking rescue from others.

CREATING A LIFE: Finding Your Individual Path
ISBN 0-919123-93-7. (2001) 160pp. *Sewn* $25
With insight and compassion grounded in the humanist side of analytical psychology, Hollis elucidates the circuitous path of individuation, illustrating how we may come to understand our life choices and relationships by exploring our core complexes.

ON THIS JOURNEY WE CALL OUR LIFE: Living the Questions
ISBN 1-894574-04-4. (2003) 160pp. *Sewn* $25
This book seeks a working partnership with readers. Hollis shares his personal experience only so that we may more deeply understand our own. It is a partnership rich in poetry as well as prose, but most of all it reminds us of the treasures of uncertainty.

Studies in Jungian Psychology
by Jungian Analysts
Quality Paperbacks

Prices and payment in $US (except in Canada, and Visa orders, $Cdn)

Bees, Honey and the Hive: Circumambulating the Centre
A Jungian exploration of the symbolism and psychology
Frith Luton *(Melbourne, Australia)* ISBN 978-1-894574-32-7. 208 pp. $30

Jung and Yoga: The Psyche-Body Connection
Judith Harris *(London, Ontario)* ISBN 978-0-919123-95-3. 160 pp. $25

The Gambler: Romancing Lady Luck
Billye B. Currie *(Jackson, MS)* 978-1-894574-19-8. 128 pp. $25

Conscious Femininity: Interviews with Marion Woodman
Introduction by Marion Woodman (Toronto) ISBN 978-0-919123-59-5. 160 pp. $25

The Sacred Psyche: A Psychological Approach to the Psalms
Edward F. Edinger *(Los Angeles)* ISBN 978-1-894574-09-9. 160 pp. $25

Eros and Pathos: Shades of Love and Suffering
Aldo Carotenuto *(Rome)* ISBN 978- 0-919123-39-7. 144 pp. $25

Descent to the Goddess: A Way of Initiation for Women
Sylvia Brinton Perera *(New York)* ISBN 978-0-919123-05-2. 112 pp. $25

Addiction to Perfection: The Still Unravished Bride
Marion Woodman *(Toronto)* ISBNj 978-0-919123-11-3. Illustrated. 208 pp. $30/$35hc

The Illness That We Are: A Jungian Critique of Christianity
John P. Dourley *(Ottawa)* ISBN 978-0-919123-16-8. 128 pp. $25

COMING TO AGE: THE CRONING YEARS AND LATE-LIFE TRANSFORMATION
Jane R. Prétat *(Providence)* ISBN 978-0-919123-63-2. 144 pp. $25

Jungian Dream Interpretation: A Handbook of Theory and Practice
James A. Hall, M.D. *(Dallas)* ISBN 978-0-919123-12-0. 128 pp. $25

Phallos: Sacred Image of the Masculine
Eugene Monick *(Scranton)* ISBN 978-0-919123-26-7. 30 figures. 144 pp. $25

The Sacred Prostitute: Eternal Aspect of the Feminine
Nancy Qualls-Corbett *(Birmingham)* ISBN 978-0-919123-31-1. Illus. 176 pp. $30

LONGING FOR PARADISE: PSYCHOLOGICAL PERSPECTIVES ON AN ARCHETYPE
Mario Jacoby *(Zurich)* ISBN 978-1-894574-17-4. 240 pp. $35

The Pregnant Virgin: A Process of Psychological Development
Marion Woodman *(Toronto)* ISBN 978-0-919123-20-5. Illustrated. 208 pp. $30pb/$35hc

Discounts: any 3-5 books, 10%; 6-9 books, 20%; 10-19, 25%; 20 or more, 40% .
Add Postage/Handling: 1-2 books, $6 surface ($10 air); 3-4 books, $8 surface
($12 air); 5-9 books, $15 surface ($20 air); 10 or more, $15 surface ($30 air)

Visa credit cards accepted. Toll-free: Tel. 1-888-927-0355; Fax 1-888=924-1814.

INNER CITY BOOKS, Box 1271, Station Q, Toronto, ON M4T 2P4, Canada
Tel. (416) 927-0355 / Fax (416) 924-1814 / booksales@innercitybooks.net